"An exquisite offering of Dave Richo's rare gift of illuminating the deepest yearnings of the human psyche—the enduring indefinables of love, meaning, freedom, happiness, and growth—that shape the flow of the ages and stages of our lives reaching for the transcendent 'more.' The skillful weaving of the eternal wisdom of poets, philosophers, and spiritual teachers with practices from modern psychology provides a deft exploration of the paradox of the ache of seeking the qualities of the 'is-ness' we already are. A timeless treasure to be deeply savored."

—Linda Graham, MFT, author of *Bouncing Back: Rewiring Your Brain for Maximum Resilience and Well-Being*

"David Richo has returned to us our very own longings. He shows us how they can reveal what it means to be truly human. The blind pursuit of 'more' is usually a corrosive fuel, but Richo demonstrates how holding our longings for more can be evolutionary. Paradoxically, we can experience them within us as 'the riches of enough.' Finally, he reminds us that we are longing for what we already have and are: What a liberating discovery! This rich harvest is conveyed with clarity and illustrated with wonderful poetry ranging from Shakespeare and Dickinson to Frost and Lowell."

—Joseph Bobrow, author of *Zen and Psychotherapy: Partners in Liberation*

"*The Five Longings* gives us a deep insight into the true nature of our human existence. Through his graceful prose, David Richo inspires us to strive toward more loving and fulfilling lives by allowing our basic longings to drive us. I recommend it to anyone on a spiritual path who wants to achieve a greater understanding of themselves, and to realize true happiness."

—Charles A. Francis, author of *Mindfulness Meditation Made Simple: Your Guide to Finding True Inner Peace*

The Five Longings

What We've Always Wanted—
and Already Have

DAVID RICHO

Shambhala
Boulder
2017

Shambhala Publications, Inc.
4720 Walnut Street
Boulder, Colorado 80301
www.shambhala.com

9 8 7 6 5 4 3 2 1

First Edition
Printed in the United States of America
⊗ This edition is printed on acid-free paper that meets the
American National Standards Institute Z39.48 Standard.
This book was printed on 30% post-consumer recycled paper.
For more information please visit www.shambhala.com.

Distributed in the United States by Penguin Random House LLC
and in Canada by Random House of Canada Ltd

Library of Congress Cataloging-in-Publication Data

Names: Richo, David, 1940– author.
Title: The five longings: what we've always wanted—and already have
/ David Richo.
Description: Boulder: Shambhala, 2017.
Identifiers: LCCN 2016033090 | ISBN 9781611803624 (paperback)
Subjects: LCSH: Self-actualization (Psychology) | Motivation (Psychology) | BISAC:
SELF-HELP / Personal Growth / General. | BODY, MIND & SPIRIT /
Inspiration & Personal Growth. | SELF-HELP / Motivational & Inspirational.
Classification: LCC BF637.S4 R57225 2017 | DDC 158—dc23 LC record available
at https://lccn.loc.gov/2016033090

For my friends
Near and dear, far and wide,
Here and dear, gone and dear

*I scarcely know where to begin
but love is always a safe place.*
—Emily Dickinson

Contents

Preface

People sometimes ask me how the idea for a new book takes shape in my mind. All my books begin the same way: I find myself struck with wonder by a topic. It is always something I am fascinated with, puzzled by, drawn to, that I start pondering deeply. My enthusiasm—and my writing skills—increase in proportion to my awe of and excitement for the topic. So my initial wonderment generally turns out to have been nothing less than grace, what I can call inspiration. In that sense, I have not really begun any book: I've only followed a muse who ushered me into it.

The origin of this book, too, happened in response to something that was always a mystery for me: our unending endless longings and why we long at all.

All my books have taught me a lot about myself. In working on these pages I have certainly learned how to identify my own longings—and to understand my interruptions of them. I am hoping that happens for you too.

I write as a spiritual practice, so I do not rush but proceed with words and feelings contemplatively. What I have written here is my way of passing on to you the results of my labor, a labor of love indeed. This book, like the others, is meant to be read slowly and meditatively, as it was written.

In the chapters that follow, I include some specific self-help practices for working with longings. In my other books, the practices have usually appeared in separate sections. This time they flowed so effortlessly from my musings that I decided to make them part of the text. I am hoping that you, like me, might thereby begin to use them to integrate insight and practice in a seamless way.

Come with me into the mysterious domain of human longing. It will sometimes seem like a Garden of Eden, sometimes like a Slough of Despond. But it will always feel like home, since every longing any of us has ever felt has contributed to making us the incomparably mysterious beings that we are.

I don't have the topic of longing totally down, as I do the times tables. The subject of longing is too vast for finality. I am still working on it in my own life, with no expectation of an end in sight. I am not a "know-it-all" as I present you with this book, only a "guess-this-much." So I won't be leading our challenging expedition, only shyly accompanying you. We are both pilgrims, together on the long Camino of lifelong longings. We find ourselves now on a path walked for centuries by many ancestors, who gladly join us on this journey of and into wonder. Our destination is the luminous sanctuary of the More we have always sought and already are.

> I have found the Grail . . . The quest for the Grail is basically nothing else than the quest for the Self . . . It is yourself that you are longing for in everything.
> —Dom Henri Le Saux, Abhishiktananda

David Richo
San Francisco, 2017

The Five Longings

Introduction

I have immortal longings in me.
—SHAKESPEARE, *Antony and Cleopatra*

We all sometimes feel there is something missing in our life. We long for whatever might make up for the lack, yet rarely with satisfactory results. How long have we longed for that which keeps evading our grasp, the fruit far out of reach, the ship that has vanished over the horizon, the lips that decline our kiss? The impossible-to-hold-on-to is precisely what arouses our deepest longings. What hoax makes us ache for what we are unable to obtain and not equipped to keep? What is it in us that makes us spread our "narrow Hands to gather Paradise," as Emily Dickinson says? Why are there existential hungers in us that don't go away, even at banquets? These are the questions we will carefully address in the pages that follow.

The fact that we have longings for the lasting in a world that is always changing is not illogical. It is a clue to the presence of something transcendent in us, that which is and seeks what's more than meets the eye in the world around us, that believes there is more to something than what it appears to be, that there is more to us than we think we are, more to our experience than we have noticed yet.

1

The words *more than* do not indicate multiplicity. This is not "more" as in "four is more than two." This is "more" as in two to the thousandth power. By the word *more* we are referring to what every longing promises: the "more" we've always wanted. We will see that it is also the "more" we were born with.

Longings can be defined as strong and lasting yearnings for that which is ultimately not fully attainable in any final way. Our longings began in early life and are with us until death. We find some fulfillment of them in the course of life, but never enough to end them. Longings are uncertain, more easily felt than defined. Women particularly seem comfortable in that domain of uncertainty. Men more often prefer things to be well defined, clearly expressed, goal-certain—which is possible in desire but not in longing. Desire is for what is clear and attainable; longing is for what is unspoken and not finally or fully attainable. The undefined style of women's longing is difficult for most men to grasp. It is quite a challenge for us men to follow Shakespeare's advice in Sonnet 23: "O, learn to read what silent love hath writ."

We all have many longings. In this book, we focus on five: love, meaning, freedom, happiness, growth. Each of these longings reveals us to ourselves, showing us what we want, what our ideals are, what motivates us, what we are really about as humans:

- Our longing for love shows us how we are meant for caring connection, not isolation. We long so deeply for a sense of belonging. The love-shaped hole inside us is filled only in those moments when we build and use our psychological and spiritual resources to feel authentic affection coming from or to us. Likewise, the longing to be seen as we are is part of the longing to be loved.
- Our longing for meaning shows us that we can never be satisfied with superficiality, because our psyches are geared to find meaning and are able to construct it from anything. The

meaning-shaped hole inside us is filled in those moments when
we trust that there is meaning in the world and in ourselves.

- Our longing for freedom shows us that we have a right to and
  capacity for the full range of human thought, imagination,
  feeling, and action. The freedom-shaped hole inside us is filled
  in those moments when we feel fully permitted to be who we
  are, no inhibitions, no compulsions, no shame. When we say
  yes to who we are, we face our biggest challenge: accessing the
  lofty freedom we never dared attempt.

- Our longing for happiness shows that our core self is nothing
  less than irrepressible joy. The happiness-shaped hole inside
  us is filled in those moments when we feel exultant about being
  ourselves, about letting others be who they are, about letting
  the world be what it is.

- Our longing to grow shows us that we are radically
  evolutionary, born to keep moving along on the journey to self-
  expression and self-expansion ultimately in the service of the
  wider world. The growth-shaped hole inside us is filled in
  those moments when we are challenged to evolve or change
  and we step up to the plate no matter what curveballs are being
  aimed our way.

We notice in all the central five longings as described above the
crucial importance of the part other people play. Longings call for
responsiveness. A thriving conscious relationship within a family,
friendship, intimate bond, is one that welcomes our longings. In
relationship all five can be held hospitably, acknowledged as legitimate, fulfilled without reluctance in whatever ways we limited
humans can do so. And we are never too ashamed to have the longings we feel or too embarrassed to ask for them to be honored.

We can survive without the fulfillment of every longing. But we
can't be fully human without *having* the five longings. For instance,
in the example of freedom: I can survive in chains, but I can't maintain my humanity if I am satisfied with being in chains. Our longings
reveal what it means to be human: to love and be loved, to live a

meaningful life, to be free, to be happy most of the time, to grow beyond our self- or other-imposed limits. The five longings are indelible imprints in all of us from our earliest life experiences and from our common human heritage as well. We all have the same longings. We all have had a different experience of how they landed in our lives, some harmoniously, some with a thud. This book lets you embrace your own longings and shows how to share them with those you trust.

The five longings are far-encompassing. Each is a *category*, a general heading comprising many spin-off longings:

Included in *love* are longings to find and give love: We seek connection, community, mutuality, belonging, companionship, support, trustworthiness, intimacy. We want an enduring sense that we are not alone, that we are cared about, that there is someone who hangs in there with us no matter what, that people, and someone special, love us unconditionally. Likewise we long to love ourselves and then to give our love to others: We might want someone special to whom we can show our love in an intimate way. On a collective level, we might long to show love far and wide by doing what contributes to the welfare of all beings.

Meaning includes a sense of purpose, some sense that our life has a goal, that what has happened to us has a significance below the surfaces we see. We also want to find fulfillment and meaning in our work, to know that it is making a difference to us and to the world around us. Likewise, we long to find a depth of meaning in relationships, in life events, in nature, and in how we see and experience the world. We want to matter to others, to know that we have a meaning in their lives: "My life matters to you" is equivalent to "I matter."

Freedom includes a certitude that we have power and agency in the world, that we are not at the mercy of the inhibitions or compulsions that are obstacles to our being free. Freedom also means personal autonomy, that others no longer have a say over how we live our lives. Our decisions are then not fear-based or made with an eye to how others might react to our choices. We long for the freedom to live in accord with our own deepest needs, values, and wishes with no obligation to design our lives to fit others' approval. We long to be free of attachments that bind us too tightly, of perspectives that narrow us, of patterns that limit us, of old unresolved issues that constrain us. We want to set our lively energy free as we would a colt from a narrow stall. We indeed stall our moment of liberation when we remain caught in archaic, though often comforting-because-familiar, habits.

Happiness includes longings for an enduring sense of safety and security in life and relationships. Our experience of happiness includes both lively joy and inner peace. This peace is composed of balance, harmony, equanimity, ease, centeredness, groundedness, a sense of flow. Inner peace gives us the capacity for contentment. We can be satisfied with the way things turn out, with what we are and have—even when it is not perfect or complete. This peace is so sturdily in us that fear, no matter its magnitude, cannot cancel or even reach it. Instead, it has become lively joy; we are *glad* to be just as we are.

Growth, on the other hand, refers to a longing to go beyond what we have and are, to develop, to evolve, to strive for more. Our growth challenges are not about contentment but about widening our world. We are built for stretching beyond our habits and constraints, for becoming bigger than safety and security allow. Deep down, we long for that which will shock us out of our self-satisfaction, interrupt our routine, hurl us into perilous territory, make our secure position precarious, put our hearts on the line. The longing for evolving-through-changing is the drive to be more than we are now, to unfold rather than fold up. Our longing for psychological growth moves us toward building self-esteem, forming healthy relationships, and resolving inner conflicts. Our longing for spiritual growth moves us toward enlightenment, love, and compassion for ourselves and all beings.

Unfolding is a form of moving. Our longings send us on a quest. We long and then we go out looking for what we long for. The five longings are exactly that which make our lives a heroic journey: We are ignited to find unconditional and universal love even when we have love right here at home. We seek a depth experience of meaning though our life has meaning just where we are. We seek an unprecedented expanse of personal freedom even if we enjoy a reasonable degree of civil liberty. We look for happiness in relationships though we have been happy in our family home. We choose a changing world of bigger challenges than any we have faced so far.

A quest is precisely about this combination of having something already but seeking more too. In Plato's dialogue on the nature of friendship, *Lysis,* we hear Socrates say, "Desire, love, and longing are directed at what is akin to oneself." In other words, we are longing for what we already have. *We are longing in daily life for what we already and always are in our inner essence.* A longing is thus not simply a treasure hunt; a longing emerges from a treasure deep within. That inner treasure contains five radiant gems: love, meaning, freedom, happiness, growth. This is what is meant in our subtitle about how our longings are fulfilled already. We will also soon consider *how,* that is, in what way they are fulfilled in daily life. The five longings are not goals; they abide in our true nature all the time. However, they are not in us like canaries in a cage we can easily see into. The five longings are in us like fish that swim in deepest waters, hard to catch, and hard to hold onto if caught. In the chapters that follow, we will learn how to trust their presence in us and how to build some angling skills as well.

We hear so much these days about being present. True presence happens in the present, that is, in this moment only. Thus it, too, like the fulfillments of longing, includes impermanence, a central Buddhist teaching. Given transience, true presence to our deepest longings really means continual relay between touching in and letting go, a way of respecting impermanence yet not giving up on yearning either. The problem is that we are sometimes trying to grasp the ungraspable. Not even this inclination has to be a source of despair, however. We recall the encouraging words of Hubert Benoit in *The Supreme Doctrine:* "It is precisely the fruitless attempt to seize the unseizable . . . which results in . . . awakening."

All of us have looked to others for the fulfillment of our longings. All of us have sometimes been successful, sometimes not. Yet, even in our deepest disappointment we find we can awaken to the truth about ourselves and others. We can then adjust the way we seek fulfillment and our expectations about it. To make that adjustment is to say yes to reality—a gargantuan task for many of us.

Our longings are not like heavy chunks of ice in our hearts. They are like flowing water in our souls. They find their way into all the nooks and crannies of our being. They build up pressure and let pressure out. They keep finding openings beneath the visible surfaces. Most of all, they resist damming. Tara Brach tells us why:

> Our longing carries us to the tender and compassionate presence that is our awakened nature.
>
> —*Radical Acceptance*

1

Our Longing for More

The more we love, the more we long to love. . . . Our whole life is nothing but longing.

—ANONYMOUS, *The Cloud of Unknowing*

Our innate longings remind us that it is not wrong to want more out of life or to refuse to be satisfied with a life of less. Longings are carefully drawn maps of our needs, our drives, our hopes, our challenges, our fears, of who we are, of who we can be. Let's look at each of these:

Our longings are vital *needs* for what we require in order to grow. We long for what we instinctively know is necessary for our personal development. In order to be fully human, for instance, we need love, meaning, freedom, happiness, and challenging experiences that help us evolve. These needs began in early life. Every one of the five longings hearkens back to our childhood needs, wishes, and dreams. As adults we ask ourselves how well our childhood environment helped fulfill our longings—or at least made room for them. *Our longings were never signs of neediness, only of our full humanity pressing for recognition.*

Our longings are *drives*, inner urges based on our needs. We have drives for food, shelter, and other necessities of survival. We also have drives for more than survival. What helps us thrive are precisely the goals of the five longings. Our drives are based on motivations to reach certain ideals. Each of the five longings is an ideal we strive for, a value we cherish and want to fulfill.

Our longings are *hopes*. Regarding the five longings, we hope for love; we hope there is meaning in dreadful or puzzling events; we hope for free rein in our life choices; we hope for peace within ourselves and among nations; we hope to grow beyond our limits, both those that are self-imposed and other-imposed. Having no longings left in our hearts would make life superficial, a plunge into despair indeed.

Our longings are *challenges*. Each asks us to step up to the plate in a way that threatens our comfort level. In every longing there is a call to change. That makes longings scary to have and to pursue. Some of our longings are for a change in how things are or who we are. We are then faced with some inner contradictions: We may long to be what others are, or what we think they are. On the other side of that coin is regret about who we are now. We might long for how things were in the past as we remember it. That can be illusory since longing is imaginative and creative and may redesign the world we came from. Our longing for the past can depict it in colors that captivate us in the present. Yet, the original colors may never have been quite so vivid.

Our longings also reveal our *fears*. Each of our longings can scare or stymie us. Most of us are ambivalent about longings. We might have gone through so many disappointments that our longings now put us on guard. We therefore prevent ourselves from fulfilling our longings—often unaware that we are doing so. In addition, we may have received messages telling us we do not deserve to have our longings fulfilled, or even to have them at all.

Our longings are *descriptions* of who we really are. We find our distinctive identity in what we long for, how we long, and why we long. A desire for a Hershey's chocolate bar is for the same product no matter who wants one. A longing is different in everyone. The love one person longs for is unique to her and so is her version of meaning, freedom, happiness, and growth. This uniqueness is how longings reveal who we uniquely are. Using an analogy, we might say there are five continents on Planet "Me." Like all continents, each is unique, yet all are related.

Likewise, the significance of longings changes according to the phase of life we are in. So does the manner in which we feel satisfied by them. For example, in college freedom might have meant uninhibited experimentation, while in motherhood, freedom involves applying our unique form of parenting and maintaining our individual identity while parenting responsibly.

It is true that longings are not fully attainable or lasting in their fulfillment—they can only ever be somewhat fulfilled and then only temporarily. However, it turns out that such limitation is a feature only of the palpably conscious dimensions in us: physical, mental, sensate, emotional. At a spiritual level, in our deep being beyond our ever-changing ego, more is going on. In our identity beyond personality, personal history, and varying feeling states, all five longings are sitting mindfully in us as lively energies. We seek to fulfill the five longings, yet they actually are filling us. Love, meaning, freedom, happiness, and growth are five *qualities* in our higher self. "Higher" refers to our identity beyond ego. Our ego, on the other hand, is focused on that which is different about each of us. The higher self is the same in all of us—why we can say we are all one. Coded into us is an impulse to actualize this wholeness. The five longings describe that impulse, always emergent, never finalized, yet we are always also whole. This is the mysterious path of a longing, already here and always on a journey: "what we've always wanted— and already have."

The five qualities, always alive within us, emerge as longings we seek to fulfill in the world around us. In other words, longings are the *echoes* of our inner wholeness. We are trying to act out with others something that is already fully accomplished in the depths of our being. Deep within ourselves we are love, have meaning, are free, are joyous, are evolving. To use an analogy, we are doing what Christian belief says that God does: God is love *and* seeks it from

us. Mystically speaking, both God and we are *seeking what we are.*
Sri Ramakrishna expresses it well: "O longing mind, dwell within
the depth of your own pure nature. . . . Your naked awareness alone,
O mind, is the inexhaustible abundance for which you long so
desperately."

We don't easily access these qualities of our "own pure nature."
Some of us don't even believe we are and have them. Our self-doubt
gets in the way. Nonetheless, growth in self-esteem can help us reach
our inner riches. Advancing in spiritual consciousness can help us
appreciate them as graces. This book attempts to usher us in both
those directions.

Just as the five longings are the qualities of our higher self, they
are also the attributes of our psychological self. Love, meaning, freedom, happiness, and growth are what our individual lives, relationships, and selves consist of. Each longing houses and awakens a part
of ourselves. Thus, we gain psychological health and self-esteem
as we:

- appreciate our longings as natural ingredients of any fully
  human life;
- let go of blaming ourselves or others when our longings are not
  met all the time;
- say yes with equal thanks to the dividends of fulfillment we
  receive, be they limited or abundant.

With practice, we can create a holding environment for our longings. In that accepting and hospitable atmosphere, we hold our longings lightly yet firmly. Then we appreciate times of fulfillment. It is
also acceptable to us that our longings are not being fulfilled right
here, right now, or all the time. Instead, we are continually on *serene*
lookout for opportunities to find some fulfillment. In relationships,
this satisfaction with "some" helps us not expect or demand too much
of one another. Paradoxically, as we will see, this will be precisely
how our relationships begin to foster the fulfillment of all five longings.
Acceptance of what is fosters evolution into what can be.

Living with paradox—not giving up on attaining the un-attainable—is what gives us depth. Regarding the unattainable, Gordon Allport, in *Becoming,* wrote of healthy psychological integration: "Salvation comes only to him who ceaselessly bestirs himself in the pursuit of objectives that in the end are not fully attained." The fact that "salvation"—fulfillment and integration—can happen *along with* unfulfilled pursuits is the paradox of our human story.

Longings are open-ended and thus inexhaustible: We find ourselves in experiences and bonds that just can't be fully understood, let alone satisfied fully. We never love or are loved enough, once and for all, for a lifetime. Likewise, we will always seek more meaning, freedom, happiness, and growth. So longings can help us settle into the realization that there are no final answers or total satisfactions. We then recalibrate our expectations of ourselves, others, and the world. What a quandary life is: We can't end a longing yet we can't let go of it either. No wonder we are people with such agonizing heartaches and such bewildering feelings. Yet, the fact that we and the whole cosmos are incomplete is precisely what makes us long for what it takes to survive and thrive:

- Without a yearning for love we would not fulfill the need for connection that is necessary for our survival.
- Without a sense that our life and life itself has meaning we would have no goals, no purpose, no dreams, no ideals—all of which drive us to be creative.
- Without freedom to be ourselves we would never emerge into our full identity or fulfill our unique potentials, the public appearance of our wholeness.
- Without inner peace we would be bottomless pits of neediness lost in the stress that harms our health and well-being.
- Without challenges assailing us we would not expand ourselves, swell to our full dimensions, launch ourselves on the expedition that a life is designed to be.

Longings thus reveal the human psyche in its fullness. Our hearts are longing-shaped after all, though our longing-shaped hearts are destined never to be completely filled. It is easy, therefore, to understand why humans are so enamored of the possibility of heaven. We want a place where all longings are utterly, fully, and finally fulfilled—and we don't mind waiting a lifetime to get to it.

Here are some affirmations that can help us contact the place in us where our five longings reside as qualities of our inner world while we still feel them as longings echoing into the world around us:

I let myself feel how loved and loving I am.
I am grateful that I am loved and loving.
I hold my longing to be loved and loving with openness for what
    more may happen.

I cherish the meaningfulness of my life and of all that happens.
I am grateful for how meaningful my life is.
I hold my longing for meaning with openness for what more may
    reveal itself.

I enjoy my own liberty.
I am grateful that I am free.
I hold my longing for freedom with openness for what more
    may be.

I contact the joy that remains in me always.
I am grateful for the joy within me.
I hold my longing for happiness with openness for what more
    may come to be.

I tap into my ongoing evolutionary impulse.
I am grateful that I am always evolving toward more love, wisdom,
    and healing.
I hold my longing to keep evolving with openness to what next
    may bloom.

I am an ongoing experiment in love, meaning, freedom, happiness, and growth. I trust that these are ineradicable capacities in myself. At the same time, as longings, they are ever unfolding, ever innovating, ever renovating—the style of our whole evolutionary world.

Why We Will Always Long

We will always long because we are always evolving. Our longings mimic the evolution of the universe: ever complete yet ever going for more. Evolution likewise means both transcending and including. Nature goes beyond what went before while holding on to what has worked. We, too, in our longings, transcend where we are and at the same time are what we were before and are what we will be.

At the most basic level, our personal evolution is about how we, like all things, can adapt to environmental changes. More than that, we are evolution conscious of itself, so we can also advance in skills to caretake the world around us. Each of the five longings is a contributor to this conscious evolutionary impulse in us:

- Love as connection leads to cooperation.
- A sense of meaning in life makes us more likely to take it seriously.
- We cooperate and respect the web of life best as free beings who want everyone else to be free too.
- Our happiness grows as we feel ourselves to be effective in cocreating a world of justice, peace, and love.
- Our urge to grow is precisely what it takes for evolution to be what it is, development and progress.

The evolutionary drive in us also explains why we long for that which eludes our grasp. We are geared to grow, expand, be more than we are, orient ourselves to an emerging future. *What makes us keep wanting what we know we can never get enough of, or have in our possession once and for all, is nothing less than our evolutionary nature.* Each of us is an incarnation of evolution inciting us to join its ever-onward, ever-enlarging, ever-deepening progression. Without longings for more we would be left behind in the desert of Going Nowhere, where our wildest human possibilities hit the dust.

We understand that longings are sometimes fulfilled but never finished. In a longing we want more but not because of a deficiency; we want more because more keeps opening to us and from us as fulfillment occurs. This is also a quality of evolution: a continuous unfolding into more than what had been before, with no final outcome. Emergent properties keep appearing and enacting themselves into being. In a world like this, our personal longings for more-than-what-has-been are ways of honoring the onward urges we were born with. Our yes to the fact that there will be no final perfect version of ourselves or of anything is honoring the fact of impermanence.

The word *continuous* also applies both to evolution and to longings. This is because in both instances a moment of advance or fulfillment leads not to a final destination but to a new threshold. We find not an end but a next step. Once again, we see how the heroic journey is a way of describing our evolutionary urge.

Evolution includes challenge and responsibility if it is to be conscious, deliberate, effective. We humans have an enormous capacity for abusing what has been entrusted to us. We are sometimes inclined to trash our planet rather than take care of it. We are sometimes apt to harm our neighbors rather than show them respectful love. Thus, in a positive evolutionary movement each longing brings with it a rallying cry to tend the world around us. Spiritual practices help us respond:

- We do not simply seek love, we show it unconditionally and universally. Our longing leads us beyond our near and dear to planetwide loving-kindness and compassion.
- We look for meaning in all that happens, especially in what comes unbidden. We respect the significance of every individual person. We engage in meaningful work and

relationships with a respectful sense of their depth, import, impact.

- We support programs and laws that guarantee the freedom of others. We want to root out prejudice in ourselves and welcome diversity. We also let go of our ego's inclination to be controlling in our relationships. We seek partnership, not domination. Likewise, we do not let others control us.
- We aspire to happiness not only for ourselves and those close to us but for those we dislike also. In our loving-kindness practice we ask for happiness for all beings worldwide. We are no longer selective.
- Our longing to grow both psychologically and spiritually does not end with us but rather opens us to caring about the growth and welfare of everyone. We look for ways to be of service so that all of us can progress along the path to justice, peace, and love.

We now see that evolution articulates the impulse to find and be more. We are not content with anything small and limited; we want what expands us. Giacomo Leopardi, the nineteenth-century poet and philosopher, wrote, "Human discontent is proof we are made for the Infinite." Longing is a spiritual impulse since "more" means transcendent, a higher power than ego. We therefore long for more than any fulfilled desire can satisfy. We recall what Emily Dickinson at age fifteen wrote to her close friend Abiah Root about "an aching void in my heart which, I am convinced, the world can never fill."

> There is a god in us who, stirring, kindles us.
> —OVID, *Fasti VI*

Something Gets Us Going and Keeps Us Going

We were born with the five longings tugging at our hearts. Each of these at some time became activated by circumstances and people. Each day we brush up against one or all of the five longings. We also experience times when none of the five is being fulfilled. Here is an example from my own experience. I was happy to have lunch at a restaurant with Jeff, a scientist friend. Being in his company felt like a loving experience. The conversation was challenging and meaningful, providing freedom for me to express my opinions and be myself. Thus, all five of the longings were being fulfilled in that hour and a half. When I left on my bicycle, everything went into reverse: I did not feel loved by the drivers of autos on the city streets. The ride was not particularly meaningful or joyous. I was not fully free but on guard for danger. And finally, I was certainly challenged by the traffic but not in a way that helped me grow and evolve, only to help me survive the contest and arrive home safely. Fortunately, whenever my ride takes me through Golden Gate Park, all bets are off and the negatives delightfully turn into positives.

The universe indeed continuously steps into our life and presents catalysts and triggers for each of our longings. These are forms of synchronicity since just the right people and experiences come along at just the right time so that any or all of the five longings can arise or find fulfillment. When did the trigger-synchronicities begin?

Our longing for *love* was awakened in infancy, when we felt instinctive needs for the main elements of love: attention, acceptance, appreciation, affection, allowing. These five *A*'s were not in the category of our need for a pacifier or a bottle. They outlived weaning. Indeed, they became the longings we carried into our fantasy life, especially in adolescence. They were also the needs we brought to our partners in adult relationships. They were not like the need for a tricycle, which could be once and for all fulfilled. They were like the need for food, unending and ever beginning anew, no matter the most recent satisfaction. As we keep noticing, all five longings are like this; what we deeply want goes on being needed even when and after we have found it. This is why longings are so extraordinarily mysterious.

Our longing for *meaning* began when we wondered why things happened as they did, why people and the world were as they were. We might also have wondered who we were beyond what our parents, school, religion, and society were trying to make us into. We kept looking for meaning no matter how much of it we found— and we continue to do so. The gift of an actively working imagination has us sometimes making meanings, sometimes discerning meanings.

Our longing for *freedom* was triggered on that first day we felt inhibited and controlled. We wanted to be released from the injunctions and demands of others, to be free to be ourselves and to choose what fit us best. We longed for a time when we could be on our own, be free to be only who we were. We still and will always want that. We also notice again and again how limited our liberty is when we are under the spell of our habits, addictions, compulsions, fears.

Our longing for *happiness* goes back to our first experience of it or to some first unhappiness we wanted to end. We kept wanting to be happy and content. We still keep looking for and finding new ways of being happy. We look for the relationships and circumstances that bring happiness. Yet, we are sometimes baffled by how long we stay in relationships and circumstances that are unhappy—an example of our ambivalence about the fulfillment of this longing.

Our longing for *growth challenges* began when we were bored by a lack of stimulation, both at home or school. We wanted more out of life, more from others, more from our activities, more from ourselves. That holds true throughout our lives, since there is an ineradicable evolutionary impulse in us to keep going on and keep moving beyond where we are. We are intrigued by how our reach extends beyond our grasp, how our sight takes us beyond where our legs might carry us. At the same time, conflicts and crises have come and still come along, all by themselves. They are graces ultimately since they present us with opportunities to evolve.

The original triggers might have been blunted by people and experiences that made us doubt the importance and legitimacy of our longings. The longings that have lasted are banners of spiritual

victories because they survived so many forces bent on subverting them. They have remained in us like unimaginably rich booty from battles long fought, some lost, some won.

No matter what went wrong in the past, the five longings are still being activated by people and events in our daily life. Here is a brief summary of our longings and what might trigger or activate them now:

Longing	*Catalyst*
Love	Those who love us and those whom we love—not limited to those we know but can include all beings
Meaning	Our questions, our whys, our wonder, our imagination, our curiosity
Freedom	Our need for independence, autonomy, openness to innovation
Happiness	Our first and later experiences of it
Growth	Challenges, conflicts, crises, joys, receiving the five *A*'s, synchronicities

What All Five Longings Have in Common

The five longings have some elements in common with one another. They also relate directly to other areas of our psychological and spiritual life:

- Each of the five longings is a component of our survival: We can't survive without caring connections and collaboration. Our motivation to honor nature and work for a better world would not thrive without a sense of their meaningfulness. Our life here would be defeating and debilitating if we did not have freedom of movement and choice. Our existence would not be worthwhile without happiness. Our innate drive to grow beyond our usual limits thrives on our engaging in evolution consciously.

- All five longings have this quality of physicality. Our body longs, not just our mind. Every longing has a feeling tone, a bodily resonance. We have a *sense* of how we want to be loved, experience meaning, freedom, happiness, and growth. Longings are not simply mental, as wishes might be.
- Each longing is linked to all the other longings. To yearn for one is to yearn for the other four at the same time. For instance, we can't long for love without also wanting meaning, freedom, happiness, growth. All five form a unity. The best symbol of the five longings is a single five-pointed star.
- Each of the five longings requires the others to be in place if it is to be fulfilled. Thus, each of the five longings leads us to the next one: We long to give and receive love. That can only happen in meaningful ways. To appreciate and act on this, we need freedom from inhibition. That liberty is a source of happiness since it is so releasing. In this entire sequence we find manifold ways to grow and evolve. Beginning with any one of the five, the others have to follow in its train.
- Our ways of giving and receiving love, the five *A*'s—attention, acceptance, appreciation, affection, allowing—have exactly the same qualities that longings have: They are not totally expressible in words; they are enduring even when found so unfulfillable in any final way; they are directed at what is more, that is, that which has depth and self-transcendence.
- Some people give away ownership of their longings. Our five longings are meant to be our own. We damage our self-esteem when we hand the reins over to someone else. For instance, in a relationship our partner is not meant to have power over how we can give or receive love. He or she cannot be in control of how much meaning, freedom, or happiness we have. Our toleration of this loss of our autonomy cancels our chances at growth.
- Longings are the same in all of us. But each longing is unique in how it is fulfilled. For instance, a person longs for happiness. For an introvert that longing can be fulfilled by a walk in the

woods. An extravert, on the other hand, will be delighted by a walk up Fifth Avenue in Manhattan.

- Longings are associated with grief. The word *pining* specifically refers to that element of a deep longing. Grief is associated with longing because any longing implies absence, a missing piece. Something we want is not available to us in any full or final way. Grief is also like longing because both can last a lifetime. A longing is like an inconsolable grief—which follows the loss of a child, for instance. Likewise, longings carry the same burden of incompletion. They abide in us even when we find fulfillment; our deep griefs sit somewhere in our hearts even on days when we are happy.

- The five longings have a spiritual foundation, because each ultimately takes us to the essential elements of spirituality: transcendence, going beyond ego, acknowledgment of the gift/ grace dimension of life and experience.

- The qualities of longings match how Buddhism describes the self and all reality: not what it seems, evanescent even while being grasped, not standing alone but connected to everything else.

- Humans have always felt the five longings. Our longings are the thread of our human connectedness: "My longings for love, meaning, freedom, happiness, growth are not coming from me but through me from my human lineage. And my longings link me to everyone on earth today."

- The five longings are both individual and collective. In Buddhist teaching *bodhicitta* refers to the awakening in us of a longing to help all beings find liberation, enlightenment. In bodhicitta we hold all five longings not only for ourselves but for everyone.

- Longings are not reactions to what has attracted us over the years. We came upon the five longings from peering into our own wholeness, a garden with five flowers, fully alive, blooming year-round in a ceaseless springtime. Their names are Love, Meaning, Freedom, Happiness, and Growth. It will take self-trust to believe there is such a garden inside us.

- We begin to realize how wistful our human struggle is: We are full of not fully attainable yearnings while deep down they are fully fulfilled. At the same time, we can't make the fulfillments of our longings happen at will at any time. Each one takes the cooperation of others and a grace from a source beyond ourselves.

As practices, there are at least three pathways that might yield us a deeper understanding of our mysterious longings, all coincidentally found in *Walden* by Henry David Thoreau:

- When we are wayfarers without a compass in a forest of longing, we can trust that a path will appear: "Not till we are lost . . . do we begin to find ourselves and realize where we are and the infinite extent of our relations."
- Our deepest longings reveal themselves in conscious silence. We can sit with our longings in contemplative silence and notice what may come to us: "You learn that if you sit down in the woods and wait, something happens." This quotation also reminds us that longing has an element of waiting, so patience is a requisite for opening to whatever fulfillment might come to us.
- We can try new experiences and then notice which ones arouse our enthusiasm, the fervor that accompanies and identifies a longing when it comes into sight. We then find more than we ever imagined: "I learned this, at least, by my experiment: that if one advances confidently in the direction of his dreams, and endeavors to live the life which he has imagined, he will meet with a success unexpected in common hours."

Something in every longing calls me to be and show the More that is in me. This means divesting myself of costumes, seeing through my self-deceptions, relinquishing my evasions. To ex-pose myself so that my true self appears in all its tatters and glories: this must be what it meant by awakening.

2

Longings, Desires, Addictions

Yield to the willow
All passions,
All desires of your heart.
—BASHŌ, translation by Asatarō Miyamori

Usually the words *desire* and *longing* are used interchangeably. Actually the dictionary shows them to be different. A desire is "for an object or goal that can be described and is fully attainable," for example, desire for a car or a college degree. A longing can be defined as a persistent yearning for what is distant or unattainable, for example, longing for the past. We can treat *yearning* and *longing* as synonyms.

Let's look in detail at the three main attributes of a longing that show how it differs from an ordinary desire:

- INDEFINABLE: We feel a longing for what we lack but can't adequately describe or express even to ourselves. We have only a *feel* for what we want, a sense of something missing. Though we cannot put our longing fully into words, we know instantly when even a whiff of fulfillment comes our way.

23

- ENDURING: A longing, unlike an ordinary need or desire, continues even during and after we receive some satisfaction of it. A longing can't be fulfilled completely, once and for all. In addition, we can't hold on to whatever gratification we are lucky to find. Yet, paradoxically, we certainly do hold on to our longings. Indeed, our deepest longings endure without interruption throughout our lives, even though we realize that fulfillment is always only *some,* never *all.*
- MORE: We are always after more, not in the sense of quantity but in the sense of depth. We long for something beyond the usual, deeper than the ordinary. We might long for an abiding, imperturbable inner peace, for instance, not just a stress-free day. We might long for the freedom to make choices that widen our narrow upbringing, not just freedom to reside out of state. We long to be truly seen in an intimate relationship, not simply looked at. We want more, something deeper than what comes from the fulfillment of desires.

All three elements have one thing in common: There is no finality. There is no final definition; there is no final fulfillment; there is no final far-enough. We fulfill our longings only in provisional or temporary ways, in moments, from time to time, here and there, willy-nilly. Yet, though we can't fulfill our longings in an enduring way, we can appreciate the times when they are somewhat fulfilled. We can learn to let that be enough. We can accept the fact that even though we can't fulfill longings fully, we can hold them fully. Rather than be settled and done with, our longings can then simply settle in us. We find the curious and unusual serenity of having and not having at the same time, the essence of elusiveness but also the essence of contentment. Then the gentle holding of our longings, becoming intimate with them, brings its own ongoing satisfaction. Our longings, securely encased in our inner world, become like old, cherished pictures in an heirloom locket.

We are sometimes imprecise in distinguishing "needs," "desires," and "longings." We might say, "I long for some time off," when we are more accurately referring to a desire for it. To see the difference, we can begin with an understanding of need. A need is a requirement, something necessary for the achievement of a particular goal. When we experience a need, it usually translates into a want, the equivalent of a desire. Some needs are immediate; some are ongoing. An immediate need is short lasting. This is a desire. An ongoing need is lifetime lasting. This is a longing.

An immediate need is one that can be fully and finally fulfilled. For instance, on a cold night I need an extra blanket and want to find one. An immediate need has led to a want or desire, and once I have found the object of my need, it is totally and finally fulfilled. I may need a blanket on another night, but that will be a new experience, not connected to my former night's need. Some desires are not based on needs: "I desire a ruby ring." I have a desire, but it shows what I *want*, not what I need.

A desire can represent a craving in the present moment that is mostly physical. This is a hankering, a yen. These words refer to a desire that hangs on, occupies our minds, and is felt mainly in our bodies. Each desire ends once it is fulfilled. For instance, I might say that I desire an ice-cream cone right now and even say, "I can already taste it." In this instance, I feel my want physically. When it is fulfilled, I no longer feel it. That same sequence holds true for my desire for the ruby ring, except that, somewhere in the sequence, I have to come up with a lot more money to fulfill that desire!

A desire may keep us frustrated or anxious until we have it: "I keep thinking of the ring I want and I feel as if I won't rest until I have it. I can only be satisfied by having the specific ring I want." A longing, however, is held more lightly. Therefore, we are not anxious about having a longing; we are used to having it in the landscape of our minds and hearts. A desire can only be fulfilled by the actual object: a ruby ring and not an emerald ring. That adds to the anxiety. A longing is not anxiety-provoking, because it can be satisfied suitably, though only temporarily, by less than all we wanted, a small taco of love rather than the whole enchilada.

Let's use another example. We have an ongoing need for human warmth. This is a longing. When someone is loving toward us, the need is being fulfilled for that moment. Yet, we keep needing the warmth of human love all our lives. A longing is only for what can be held and not kept, leased but not owned. Using another example, a longing for time in nature can take us to Yosemite, but we can only visit it, not possess it. That existential predicament is part of the very definition of a longing—and, as we shall see, it is what gives us depth as people.

A desire can be aimed at what is abstract or concrete: We desire a car; we desire a relationship. We long only for what is abstract: We long for freedom of choice in our daily life; we long for deeply felt love and intimacy in a relationship. Regarding relationship, here is another example of the difference between desire and longing: You are looking forward to your lover's return. You might say, "I am longing for him to come back." This is actually a desire. You know who he is and what his return will look like; you desire his concrete presence in your space. Longing, happening with the desire, is occurring at a much more profound and elusive level. It is not about his knocking at the door or standing in your room. What you long for is the unexplainable and unique *feeling* that happens between you when you are together, a feeling only he can ignite and sustain. Your experience will be like other returns of his, and yet it promises to have its own special flavor this time. That bodily sense, ineffable, known only in the moment it happens, not able to be told or held on to, is what makes it a longing.

Desire is aimed at what is totally outside ourselves, for example, candy. But our five longings reflect what is already inside us as rich components of our inner life. When we desire, we are looking at what attracts us from outside and we reach for what we don't have. When we long, we are looking at what attracts us because we *do* have it inside. A desire works from the outside in: we were not born with candy inside us, but once we see and taste it, we desire it. A longing works from inside out: we were born free and now we want to live out what we know is our birthright.

Longings often masquerade as desires. This is understandable since desires are easier to identify and generally easier to fulfill than longings are. For instance, we long for the kind of freedom we feel in the mountains. We might feel that as a desire to spend time in the Rockies. While hiking there, we will feel that something unnamable is being fulfilled. That is the longing that is now finding some fulfillment. The desire was fully fulfilled when we arrived; the longing is gradually fulfilled during our visit—though not finally, so we will want to return next year.

Both desire and longing are necessary in human experience. Desire takes us to a new store—with candy in it. A longing holds up a mirror to our inner treasury—with a soul in it. In all the distinctions above we notice that desire and longing are intimately related. Desire is to longing not as an apple is to an ape. Desire is to longing as an apple is to its core. Our desire for the knock on the door by the hand of a lover taps into our core longing for love. Our heart, however, once it is aglow, can hardly tell the difference.

To summarize our main points, here is a chart that lists some differences between desire and longing:

Desire	*Longing*
Is clearly describable	Can best be described as a sense of or feel for something
Interprets "more" as quantitative	Interprets "more" as transcendent
Can be concrete or abstract	Can only be abstract
Often has a quality of immediacy: "I want it now!"	Is comfortable with not having fulfillment in the present moment
Is limited to exactly this	Can vary each time, is open-ended
Can be easily and quickly satisfied	Is difficult to fulfill
Has to have it all	Permits partial fulfillment
Makes us frustrated when it is not fulfilled	Is held serenely since we are aware of the quality of impermanence in it
Is dualistic: "I desire this."	Is a unitive experience: "I am this."

Desire	Longing
Is about obtaining an object, attaining a goal, or having an experience	Is about experience only
Seeks more and more	Opens into what is deeper and deeper
Can be superficial	Always has depth
Comes and goes, ends with finding what we wanted: desires happen throughout the day	Endures all our lives no matter how often it finds some fulfillment: longings are lifelong
Is based on an immediate need	Is based on an ongoing need
Refers to Maslow's "deficiency needs"	Refers to Maslow's "growth needs"
Is in the foreground of our minds	Can be in immediate focus but is mostly in the back of our minds
Can become addictive	Is not vulnerable to addiction
Operates on the level of "The more you get, the more you want."	Operates on the level of "The more you get, the more deeply you appreciate it. You then want a deeper experience of it next time."
Is often paired with fear or anxiety: we fear not finding what we want	Is usually paired with grief because we can't be fully and finally satisfied when we do find some fulfillment
Is for something external and resides in our body-mind-ego as a need or want that is not yet fulfilled	Is an echo of what is always and already in us, often unconscious but it can become conscious in mindful moments or in mystical experiences

Here are some examples of desires/wants and how they relate to the five longings:

- We want specific people to love us; we long for a life of love.
- We want to find meaning in what happens; we long for the meaningful.

- We desire liberties; we long for liberation.
- We desire pleasures; we long for happiness.
- We want successes; we long for growth.

Both Desires and Longings Are Teachings

Aristotle, in his *Rhetoric* 1.1370, writes, "Desire is a reaching out for the sweet . . . by means of an act of imagination." Both desire and longing thrive on imagination. Thus, desires, longings, hankerings, yens all teach us how much of our thinking and wanting is based on reality and how much on illusion. They also show us that it is not necessary to align our thoughts—or longings—with reality all the time, especially if we are to be creative.

A desire is time-bound. We want something here and now, or have wanted it for a while. When we find what we want, our desire ends. A longing has no shelf life. Right now, reader, you may not want the dessert you desired last night. But you do have all five longings from last year and all the years before. They are up and running right here and now—even though each of them has found some fulfillment over the years or yesterday. In this sense, awareness of longings is an indicator of the fact that we are always living in the present. Desires, on the other hand, indicate only impermanence. Thus, both longing and desire point to Buddhist teachings. Our very being is teaching us the Dharma, the enlightened way to spiritual consciousness. The psyche with all its longings and desires is Buddha alive today and here in us. In our longings, we glimpse our Buddha nature, a realm of love, meaning, freedom, happiness, growth. In our desires Buddha is teaching us impermanence. In addition, when we long or desire *with an openness to any outcome,* a "let it be" attitude, we are free of craving. We have let go of the "must have" energy that is the cause of suffering, another Buddhist teaching.

Desire, as we are describing it here, can be directed toward what has depth, for instance to become a parent or follow a calling, both lasting. Desire can also be for what has little meaning, for instance, a hot dog, a flash in the pan. A longing, however, is only for what deepens us, a flash of the more-than-what-we-were. It is our capacity to long that reveals the spiritual world inside and around us.

Our desires are learned; we imitate others and want what they want. Advertising capitalizes on this penchant of ours. Likewise, we might do what others do, as for example, what happens when an individual falls prey to a crowd mentality. Longings, however, are our own. We may want a swimming pool because our neighbor has one. But we want love no matter whether anyone else has it or not. We long for love in the unique way we felt it that first time long ago and we want it again. In addition, we want love because it is in us and so we want to give it away and find it in return, if possible. We are thereby learning about what love is and how to share it. This applies to the other four longings as well.

A desire is either for or against something. We desire to find something or get rid of something. A longing is geared only toward finding. For example, we are aware of our brokenness. Our desire is to be fixed, to end our distress. Our longing is to work with our brokenness so that growth can happen through it. Thus, we learn from our longings about the kind of integration that leads to healing.

A desire substitutes for a longing. We will explore how this applies to addiction in the next section. Longing is about what we have wanted all along. Desire is about what we settle for in the moment. For instance, we want a sense of familiar childhood comfort, so we settle for a malted milk shake, a comfort food. We are giving up on what we really want in favor of what works for now. This same trading style can apply to our choices of partners in intimate relationships. We long for the one who will love us tenderly and we wind up with the one who hurts us. When he keeps doing it and we don't move on, we have despaired of finding a fulfillment of our longing. It is always appropriate to seek love, but if we missed out on it in childhood, we may not believe we deserve it. Our longing for healthy love remains intact, but our desire takes over and we fall for the one who looks the part but can't really measure up to it. Our ability to pick a healthy partner has been damaged, so our choice making is flawed. Our longings show us where the work of addressing, processing, and resolving awaits us. The story of our longings show us also where and how to have compassion for ourselves for all the mistakes we have made.

Wanting More, but Not Addictively

> Indeed the idols I have loved so long
> Have done my credit with the world much wrong:
> Have drowned my glory in a shallow cup
> And sold my reputation for a song.
> —*The Rubáiyát of Omar Khayyám*, translation by Sir Richard Burton

There is a fine line between wanting more, as in longing, and wanting more and more as we do in addiction. For instance, addiction to alcohol and spiritual seeking are both aimed at finding more. The difference is that in spirituality we are focused on being more, looking for a passageway to enlightenment. In addiction we are obsessed with *getting* more, an alleyway to impairment. An addiction is about escape from oneself, not about the presence to oneself that is characteristic of a longing. Since, nonetheless, both longing and addictive craving include a desire for more, what is the difference between healthy longing and insatiability?

Longing	*Insatiability*
Is invulnerable to addiction	Is a sign of addiction
Can put off gratification	Has to have it all now
Includes a capacity for contentment when some fulfillment is given	Is an inability to get enough no matter how much is given
Seeks fulfillment within connection	Seeks fulfillment in objectifying
Seeks more quality	Wants more quantity

Longing	*Insatiability*
Expands our focus in the world around us	Contracts our focus to the object of our addiction
Can hold a yearning gently in the background so it is present but does not preoccupy us	Keeps the object in the foreground so it becomes an obsession
Is open to fulfillment and keeps an eye out for when it can happen	Is a compulsive seeking and often directed to the wrong objects
Is grounded in an acceptance of reality with room for imagination	Is ungrounded, based on fantasy
Can live with a yes or a no from others	Can't tolerate a no
Goes with the flow, flexible	Has to be in control, inflexible
Maintains inner peace in both fulfillment and nonfulfillment	Remains restless even in moments of fulfillment

Addictions, coincidentally, thrive on the very same three elements of longing: they are beyond full description, continue even after satisfaction, aimed always at more. A specific example is online pornography. What the addict seeks can't fully be defined, so he goes from site to site. He is not satisfied even after some or many pleasures. He is seeking more than can be found on the screen. How ironic that the real *more* is and always has been within but is the last place we look for it.

A way to understand the connection between longing and addiction more deeply is by looking at a German word, *Sehnsucht.* This refers to longing with the sense of strongly missing someone or something. The root *Sehn* refers to a yearning and includes the concept of "tendons," implying a firmly held connection. The second half of the word refers to addictive connection (*Sucht*). However, these definitions fail to catch the exact meaning of the word *Sehnsucht.* The longing it refers to is emotional, not rational. It also

includes a recognition of the given of life that nothing is fully finished or even entirely graspable. In Sehnsucht we experience the
frustration of seeking fulfillment while knowing all along it will elude
us. The experience is further aggravated by the fact that we are
aware that we are longing but don't quite know for what. All we
know is that we keep wanting to go to a far-off and unnamed land.
We are homesick for a home we never lived in, its door intriguingly
familiar, its keys irretrievably lost.

Addiction is attached to the object of a desire. Behind that desire
might be a longing we gave up on. For instance, we give up on
finding love, so we might be seeking sex in a compulsive way. That
kind of sex offers a physical closeness that mimics love, so we con-
vince ourselves that it can stand in for what we really long for.

What does life look like when we trade longing for desire and
then become addicted to our desire? Early in life Pino gave up on
finding the five *A*'s—attention, acceptance, appreciation, affection,
allowing—the principal longings of love. Pino gave up especially on
finding meaningful touch, the *A* of affection. Instead of holding that
longing within himself and remaining open to finding some fulfillment whenever it happened to come along, Pino chose to satisfy
himself with multiple sexual encounters, intimacies but no intimacy.
Orgasm, for him, was the lure to satisfying a desire, what he turned
to when he gave up on longing.

Spending his years from age fifteen to forty-five focusing on the
frantic search for sex kept Pino in a shallow world—the kind that
houses any addiction. Pino usually felt a sense of emptiness after his
meaningless sexual encounters. Because of his childhood religious
teaching, he thought this was because of an uneasiness about doing
what was immoral. But the emptiness Pino encountered was the
vacuum created by the disregard of his true longings. Inner emotional emptiness tells us our longings are either not being met or that
they are being traded in for what desire promises to procure yet
can't deliver.

Pino's obsession with sex was ultimately a distraction from deepening himself, that is, from dedicating himself to pursuits he could

be proud of, having something to point to as meaningful, something that would lead to personal expansion or contribute to the good of others. Pino traded in his longings, what would deepen him, for desire, what gratified him.

Pino's story is touching because he was not only motivated by despair but also by fear. He noticed the requirements of true intimacy early on and they scared him. Pino used sex as a way of running from commitment. He focused on finding partners who would cater to his desires rather than the one who would identify and perhaps respond to his longings. The prospect of finding such a partner was scary, because Pino would then have had to entrust his tender longings to another human being. Vulnerability is trusting someone with our longings. In the clench of fear, we might prefer not showing them our longings—or even knowing them ourselves.

In some sexual encounters, understood by his partners as limited to sex only, Pino felt a special closeness, though it was, unbeknownst to him, one-sided. It seemed to him that the encounters contained real love, the fulfillment of his longing. Pino acted the part of an authentic affectionate lover. Then he believed his own acting. When his partners showed no interest in following up, Pino was deeply disappointed and hurt, his expectations dashed. He did not realize that the sexual events did not really have the depth he had projected into them and that he would "benefit no further than vainly longing," as Shakespeare writes in *King Henry VIII*.

Pino's sex life was run by testosterone and adrenaline, the glands of "manliness." However, Pino may someday meet a new kind of woman, one whose hugs and kisses arouse an oxytocin response. Oxytocin is a hormone produced in the hypothalamus. It gives a sense of connectedness, warmth, belonging, such as happens in cuddling. Pino will have to shift his focus from testosterone fun-sex to give more attention to the oxytocin dimension of sex-with-full-connection. The former is performance oriented; the latter is bonding oriented. In sex, both oxytocin and dopamine are released. Focusing only on testosterone-adrenaline-dopamine sex, Pino might have his first sexual-performance problem. "Oxytocin-centered sex" operates on a mechanism that will be new to Pino. He will suddenly have become an amateur. A "manly guy" like him might not be able to step up to that plate until he does some work on his regressive, habitual, and, in this new situation, inadequate, sexual response.

So many of us lose track of what we really long for as evolutionary beings: what opens and stretches us—two essential requirements for deepening ourselves. When desire or addiction rule our lives, we forfeit wonderful opportunities for opening and stretching ourselves. Recovery programs can help us find them again. We can then feel compassion for ourselves. Perhaps we finally realize that we had never learned to hold our love-longings in healthy ways. We followed only the lead of so many movies and so many of our own hormones that told us to "Go for it!" Like Pino, we hearkened to those voices, not necessarily or only in the realm of sex, but in whatever dominant focus distracted us from our authentic life goals. It could have been an addiction; it could have been a dead-end relationship or job; it could have been a contest our ego just had to win.

Pino, like his namesake Pinocchio, loved the thrills in the Land of Ice Cream. But it is not too late for him—or for you or me—to become the Pinocchio who was awakened in the belly of the hero-making whale, the one touched to wholeness by the wand of the divine feminine that makes us real.

3

How Longings Challenge Us

The whole world yearns after freedom, yet each creature
is in love with his chains; this is the first paradox and
inextricable knot of our nature.

—SRI AUROBINDO, *Thoughts and Glimpses*

For most of us, longings include ambivalence. We draw near and
run away at the same time. Our longings might have met with
cautionary messages in childhood that still resound in our psyches.
We might have been warned about not going too far or wanting too
much. We might have been told we did not have longings or that
we *should* not have any. These admonitions might have been aimed
at all five of our central longings:

- We might have been pushed away when we needed affection
  or rebuked for wanting it.
- We might have been told that our version of what is meaningful
  had to be aligned with familial or religious beliefs.
- We might have been warned to beware of freedom since we
  would not know how to set appropriate limits when necessary.
- We might have been informed that happiness could not last or
  that we didn't deserve it anyway.

- We might have been told that our development needed to be mapped out for us by authorities on the topic, not by our own sense of who we were or what we needed.

Some of us were encouraged in our longings. We came from homes that made it safe to have them. There were also home situations in which longings were encouraged too much, where the idea of fulfilling longings was given too central a role. Children in those settings might now feel entitled to have every longing fulfilled in their relationships. Yet, no matter what messages came through in childhood, each of the five longings can arouse a fear response in us now:

Love can be scary in a relationship because it involves closeness and vulnerability. Both of these can feel threatening because they require trusting someone. This will feel like walking a tightrope if we come from a history of being betrayed in relationships. Someone getting close to us can evoke a terror of engulfment even when that is not actually happening. Vulnerability can feel like allowing ourselves to be hurt or hurt again as we were before.

In attachment theory, fear of engulfment is the style of avoidant attachment. With this fear we are likely to distance ourselves from our partner. We distrust our partner's sense of appropriate boundaries, fearing she might get too close. On the other hand, fear of abandonment is the style of anxious attachment. With this fear we are likely to cling to our partner. We doubt and distrust his commitment to stay. *Our longing for love in relationships is for a secure attachment.* In a secure attachment we neither cling nor run; we trust ourselves to welcome closeness without feeling engulfed, and to allow distancing without feeling abandoned. Then we maintain boundaries in our relationships, but they are not barriers to intimacy.

Meaning challenges us because we are impelled to organize our lives accordingly. For instance, a recognition of the importance of taking a stand for ecology may entail letting go of some of our own wasteful habits. Our finding the real meaning in what someone has said to us may require us to be assertive in response, to stand up for ourselves, what can be a daunting prospect.

Freedom and happiness can arouse our fears if we have lived entirely within mainstream life and values in order to feel safe and secure. True freedom and happiness entail living in accord with values and choices that we have chosen. That can certainly include choosing a conventional life. It can also mean being marginal, or becoming a laughingstock, which may lead to rejection by those around us. To live a conventional life because it is safer than being who we really are impedes our freedom. We might be afraid to let our hair down fully, to show our true hand, to take actions that reveal our divergence from the safe majority. Such full freedom might come across as frightening possibilities for any of us. Truly liberated people are free of bondage to what society demands, nor are they swayed by people's opinions of them.

Growth means accepting challenges to expand, to go beyond our sheltered lifestyle and patterns, to live up to ideals that take us beyond our comfort zone. We are also challenged to stop blaming our parents for the shape our life has taken. Growth means, in effect, taking full responsibility for ourselves, our feelings, our choices, our plans, our regrets—all fearsome biddings when we are used to blaming the world around us.

How ironic that we fear following our longings on their journey into the depths of ourselves. What terror has burrowed into our souls that makes us avoid what would deepen us? *We fear exactly that which can free us from fear:*

- Love frees us from fear because fear excludes and love includes.
- Meaning shows us how what happens can have a purpose or be a remedy when we face it without fear.
- Freedom means letting go of inhibitions and compulsions based on fear.

- Happiness is characterized by a sense of all-rightness with ourselves and the world, which equips us bravely to face whatever might happen to us.
- A commitment to that which helps us grow is a way of facing our fears and acting in such a way that they no longer stop or drive us. Then we put less time into running from what we fear and more into moving toward what we love. That will be a heroic journey indeed.

When We Find Abundance

We sometimes receive love, discover meaning, obtain freedom, experience happiness, find opportunities to grow—in abundant ways. Yet, in the presence of such a cornucopia, we might also feel afraid and hesitant. We feel safer with what is more familiar, a smaller helping or none at all. We believe we "want it all," yet in the special moments when that happens we might freeze, misunderstand it, suspect it, fear it, flee it.

Perhaps we humans share an existential condition, an incapacity for abundance. All may be too much. In Emily Dickinson's poem, "I had been hungry all the years," we come upon this very theme. The poem tells us how she had longed for nurturance and finally the time came for her to have it in full measure. But she found herself "trembling" and could not fully partake of the banquet precisely because it was "ample" and she had become used to just a "crumb." She felt "ill and odd" in the presence of the copious fulfillment of her lifelong longing. The total availability of fulfillment actually caused the yearning to leave her altogether: "Nor was I hungry." Finally, she realized that longing is what it feels like to be "outside windows" looking in at a feast, but as soon as it becomes truly accessible, the possibility of fulfillment by it vanishes. The same theme appears often. Shakespeare speaks of this human conundrum in Sonnet 29: "With what I most enjoy contented least." Similarly Robert Frost says, in "After Apple-picking": "I am overtired/Of the great harvest I myself desired." Likewise, Naomi Shihab Nye, in "So Much Happiness," writes: "It is difficult to know what to do with so much happiness."

In another poem, "Who never wanted—maddest Joy," Emily Dickinson gives one more reason that we might pull back once our longings are "within" our "reach, though yet ungrasped." We fear that direct fulfillment of our longing might disappoint us. Holding on to the fantasy about fulfillment might be better than finding it. We fear getting too near fulfillment "lest the actual should disenthrall" us, rob us of the fiction we have held on to for so long. Indeed, a longing can give us more pleasure than its fulfillment, since a fantasy is wilder and more magical than the real thing. We won't forget the jazz singer Peggy Lee wondering, in the face of reality, "Is that all there is?"

On the other hand, longings can increase after an abundant fulfillment, especially when followed by a letdown. We recall the humorous World War I song about how difficult it will be to keep returning veterans satisfied "down on the farm after they've seen Pa-ree." This is reminiscent of what in Buddhism is called the first noble truth about reality: its ultimate unsatisfactoriness even in fulfillment. In Buddhist teaching, an inability to be satisfied is built into human nature. The same inability is built into the very nature of longings.

Is our universal experience of longing therefore a trick on us? Here is a tender response from the Anglican mystic poet George Herbert in his poem "The Pulley." God has just created a man and given him many natural gifts, but not the capacity for fulfillment by them:

> Yet let him keep the rest [of the gifts]
> But keep them with repining restlessness;
> Let him be rich and weary, that at least,
> If goodness lead him not, yet weariness
> May toss him to my breast.

The word *restlessness* is reminiscent of Saint Augustine's words in his *Confessions:* "You have made us for Yourself, O God, and our hearts are restless until they rest in You." Restlessness is evidence of longing for a reality beyond ego. Poet and saint see this as built into our very nature as human beings. In his commentary on the Psalms Saint Augustine even adds this: "A longing is a prayer. If you long without ceasing, your prayer will also be without ceasing. The continuance of your longing is the continuance of your prayer."

Yet, there are people whose capacity for satisfaction lets them rest in a sense of completion and contentment when a longing is fulfilled. We see this serene alternative described by Amy Lowell in her poem "A Decade," celebrating the tenth anniversary of her relationship with her female partner:

> I hardly taste you at all for I know your savour,
> But I am completely nourished.

In these lines, we see the poet experiencing the opposite of what happened to Emily Dickinson. Here the fulfillment of a longing happens in a fully satisfactory way: She is "completely nourished." In those two words the very definition of a longing as ultimately unfulfillable, is overturned. Our conclusion can only be that some people do indeed have the faculty of being comfortable with abundance. They have found the knack of holding a longing without becoming prey to its limitations. They are not ambivalent. They have a capacity for copiousness. A relationship offers us a threshold into that possibility when it really works and lasts. In fact, that's how we know it is really working; we feel we are in an ongoing state of love, loving, and being loved, no matter what conflicts may arise.

Likewise, with regard to the other four longings, an ongoing sense of serene plentiful fulfillment is possible. We can have an overall sense that our life has meaning even when we seem to be going nowhere. We can feel generally happy, even though we are sometimes sad or under the gun for something. We can know we are growing in many ways even when we go backward in some ways. We can feel free even when we are under an obligation to do something we would rather not do.

In our Buddha nature we are fully enlightened, but in our daily life we often act in unenlightened ways. Thus, our enlightened state turns out not to mean much for most of us. How do we find a way to experience our enlightened nature, a full fulfillment of our ancient longings? We all have Buddha nature. How can we act in accord with a Buddha mind?

- We come upon that way in moments of stillness, while ego is asleep, while thoughts are napping, while words are lost in silence.
- We arrive when we have no control over our steps, no map to follow.
- We abide in wholeness when we recognize without doubt that all that has happened, without exception, is grace, assistance on our path.
- The fulfillment likewise reveals itself in mindful presence or in mystical reverie.
- It happens when our whole life becomes an unconditional yes to what is.
- It happens when there is no "it," only wholeness.
- It happens when absolutely everything is holy.
- It is then, and only then, that we enter and stay in the sheer and ceaseless glory.

Two people have been living in you all your life. One is the ego—garrulous, demanding, hysterical, calculating. The other is the hidden spiritual being, whose still voice of wisdom you have only rarely heard or attended to.

—Sogyal Rinpoche, *The Tibetan Book of Living and Dying*

If Nothing Lasts, Why Seek? The Answer Is Yes

I hope for the best and accept what comes.

—former president Jimmy Carter, after his cancer diagnosis

Our sense of impermanence confounds our longings. The fact that they are so long standing fools us into thinking they point to something lasting. But nothing escapes the ruthless scythe of time, so longings end, so fulfillments end, so dreams for more end. Ralph Waldo Emerson, in his journal of 1840, wrote, "Always the present object gave me this sense of the stillness that follows a pageant that has just gone by." We keep noticing the grief dimension in the inevitable fact that this present moment's fulfillment so soon passes away.

A poem by the ancient Greek poet Simonides expresses impermanence, even in how each succeeding line becomes shorter than the one before:

> Being human, you can't predict what will happen tomorrow
> Nor, when someone prospers, if it will last.
> For swifter than a long-winged fly,
> Behold, a change!

The poem points to impermanence as a fact of life. The equivalent Buddhist teaching takes us one step further. Not only is it true that nothing is permanent but we bring suffering on ourselves by clinging to something as if it were permanent. We can therefore look with compassion at this tendency in us to cling and become stuck in quicksand at times. With compassion we begin to hear the teachings with soft openness rather than with hard judgment against ourselves.

One way to feel a longing without dangerously clinging is in the attitude of acceptance of any alternative: "I long for it and if I get it, I get it; if I don't, I don't. No big deal either way." This reduces our anxiety because it is a yes with equanimity to whatever the final outcome will be. Ultimately satisfaction or dissatisfaction have to become equal; in other words, we must ultimately consent to the way things are. We say yes to what is and to how we feel about it. To wish it were different is a form of suffering. *Yes* is freedom from that suffering because it is an experience of safety and security when there is none in sight. *Yes* is also what in Buddhism is called "right view," seeing things as they are in the present, defying what they seem to portend.

The yes of equanimity can coexist with healthy grief, our appropriate response to inevitable losses. A spiritual approach to life does not eliminate our feelings. In this regard we recall Zen master Sōen Shaku weeping for a friend who had died. A bystander mocked him and asked, "Aren't you supposed to be beyond reacting to losses?" Shaku replied, "It is *allowing* my grief that puts me beyond it." What a profound paradox.

Life keeps showing us that what we want or cling to doesn't last. This fact does not mean that what is impermanent is necessarily of less value than what is permanent—a common bias. The fact that something will not last can mean that it is very precious indeed, precisely because it will be with us so briefly. The Japanese celebrate such impermanence, as we see in the ritual honoring the cherry blossoms. Likewise, a Mozart concerto is temporary, but we cherish it as an experience of pure joy. Yet, we would not want it to go on forever while so many other activities and pleasures await us in a day. Likewise we know ourselves and our tendency to tire of repetition. Transitoriness is, then, not a disappointment or a deficiency. It is an invitation to appreciate impermanence and then feel gratitude for what it offers to beings like us so apt to have things cloy.

While writing this book, I visited Yosemite National Park. Standing alone there one early morning, I was gazing at a radiant rainbow around a rushing waterfall. In that moment, I felt as if all my longings, every one, were being perfectly fulfilled. I wanted nothing else; I even felt I would never want more than that. A power in nature was conferring and confirming my wholeness; there was no further need to seek or long. It also seemed that the giant trees all around were holding me in a comforting embrace. I found myself feeling the safety and security I have always looked for, from childhood until now. I was looking at, surrounded by, and was within the sacred heart of the universe. It was a powerful spiritual experience, yet it was not to last. Very soon the rainbow faded, the sun went in, a raw wind chilled me to the bone. But that moment of oneness in and with it all had been enough. I could say yes to the paradox of fullness in transitoriness. It isn't often I can allow that combination. I usually demand that the enjoyable last, not at all willing to let it go. But this time I did let go, and that made the whole experience a grace. The Great Mother had shown me her rainbow attire—and its tendency to wane, only to wax again someday somewhere else for someone else. The reality of ever-recurring seasons and cycles is earth's consoling riposte to every instance of impermanence. And today I realize that perhaps a time will come when a vanishing rainbow, a dying sun, or a chill wind will become equally as entrancing as the splendor I beheld that day.

For any of us, a comfortableness with paradox can prepare us to appreciate the passing and the lasting with equal serenity. Longing itself contributes to making that possible, because by it we keep seeking what lasts even though we know nothing does. We don't have to see that contradiction in us as foolish. It is a sign of creativity and optimism about finding something enduring in a transitory world. It can be honored as a tribute to our never giving up. We then find novel and surprising ways to hold our longings, an optimism that defies the facts at hand:

- Through many disappointments and betrayals, we stay with our longing for love and it may become an openness to finding it in ourselves or anywhere.
- Passing through events that seem so utterly meaningless, we stay with our longing for meaning and it may become a knack for discovering an ultimate significance in the here and now of what is.
- After years of inhibition and compulsion, we stay with our longing for freedom and it may become a letting go.
- From unhappy times we stay with our longing for happiness and we might find it happening without our having to search for it.
- After longueurs of stuckness, we stay with our longing for growth and soon might see ourselves evolving into all we can be.

There's actually only one thing, which is basic goodness, and it's either recognized or not recognized. What's powerful about this is that it's really saying that the basic nature of everything—any experience that we have, no matter how caught and fixated and confused we feel—if you contact it directly, I think the wording I used from Ponlop Rinpoche was, "Rest in the rawness of the energy and it will transform by itself. It will return to basic goodness." If you're looking for basic goodness and you're very angry, or you're looking for basic goodness and you're full of self-pity or whatever emotion you're feeling, you're not going to find it by getting rid of what you're feeling—you have to find it right in the feeling itself. . . . It is pretty much basic Buddhism that it's never about getting rid of.

—PEMA CHÖDRÖN, Making Friends with Yourself (online course)

The real victory for me was when I was able to recognize my profound inner experience of *goodness as the core and foundation of all reality* . . . but it is still and always . . . a surrender of *the idea of goodness for which I long*—instead of the actual goodness that is given.

—RICHARD ROHR, "The Trap of Perfectionism"

How We Let Others Know What We Long For

All my longings lie open before you, Lord; my sighing is not hidden from you.

—Psalm 38:9

Longings do not yield easily to words. Nor do they like direct sunlight. And they certainly stutter when it comes to asking for fulfillment from someone. This book, nonetheless, proposes a radical practice: noticing and asking for fulfillment of our longings. To incur such a risk takes a willingness to be awkward and vulnerable, giant steps toward psychological and spiritual health.

Now we can look in detail at the main two ways of sharing our longings: noticing and expressing. These can serve as practices that help us to know our own longings clearly and to bring them to others safely.

Noticing

We begin very simply by recalling our fantasies. Longings are hidden in each of them. What we always wanted, what our daytime reveries are about, give us clues about what we long for in our hearts. They are not to be taken literally; each is a metaphor for a larger yearning. For instance, a sexual fantasy may cloak a longing for a specialized kind of holding we never dared pursue, mention, or even admit to ourselves that we want.

Now we describe our longings in a journal. This means more than simply naming them. It is also important to see the context in which they arose in us. We can jot down the origin of each. We may often recall a longing going all the way back to childhood. We ask ourselves if it was welcomed in our family home or given the hospitality portrayed by the five *A*'s. These five *A*'s feel real only when they are shown both in word *and* deed.

Our longings might also have arisen in an environment that inhibited, abridged, denied, or crumpled them. For instance, we may have been imprinted with messages from early life—home, school, church, society, peers—that forbade us to know the tender parts of ourselves. We were not encouraged or perhaps not even allowed to ask directly for the human warmth we wanted. That convinced us that we had no right to ask, that we were irreparably undeserving, that there was no hope for our longing. None of this has to stop us now. We can overwrite negative messages and lay down new neural pathways in our brain, ones that replace the negating ones. Recent important research in the brain's neuroplasticity has shown us many ways to reprogram ourselves. For instance, one way to override our negative internalized messages is to voice-over them with affirmations like the ones listed below. We can also recite the affirmations daily, paying attention to the feelings they bodily evoke in us. We may soon notice that challenges to the affirmations start showing up here and there. We face them and notice how the use of the affirmations can redirect us to new behaviors no longer in the grip of fear.

- I am free to ask for what I need.
- I have a right to speak my piece.
- I deserve to be heard.
- I say yes to the fact that some people won't want to hear from me or listen to me. I let go of taking this personally. I keep trying or, when appropriate, let go while being respectful and nonretaliatory.
- I trust my longings as clues to a larger life than ego in me.
- The universe—higher power, God, Buddha nature—supports me with empowering grace.

Expressing

The second step in letting others know what we long for is expressing our longing to them directly. We practice this first with friends and confidants. In doing so, we are attempting to share our deepest yearnings in whatever faltering words we have found so far, no matter how wobbly. They do, after all, come from the most sacred and sensitive precincts of our tender hearts. We do not speak of our longings to anyone who might laugh at them, say we are asking for too much, or scorn us for sounding entitled. Longings are too important to be suppressed just because they are scoffed at. All that matters at this stage is that we hear ourselves articulate them and have them witnessed by a trusted person. We do not declare our longings to manipulate a response but only because they are there in us and require a declaration and a hearing.

In the next step, the stakes are raised. We tell our longings to our partner, family member, or someone close to us. Here we will feel vulnerable because telling is asking. We have to be able unconditionally to trust the person we approach with our precious longings. We are letting him or her know what we want, who we are, at the deepest level of our being. This is not simply stating a desire, for example, "Kiss me." We are opening our heart of longing and our heart is asking, "The kiss I long for is not lips to lips but heart to heart. I long for the presence, the nearness of you in a closer way than ever."

Some of us have partners who do not yet have the depth it takes to see or understand a longing. It might take time to help them understand. Here are some opening gambits into each of the five longings and how we might express them to someone who cares about us, the someone worthy of receiving them but perhaps not adroit at fulfilling them.

Love: We let the other know what feels like love to us. One way to do this is to talk about each of the five *A*'s. We explain in detail what feels to us like attention, acceptance, appreciation, affection, and allowing.

Meaning: We explain how experiences become meaningful to us when we talk about them together, reflecting on how they have affected us. We point out that appreciation from the other gives us a sense that what we do has meaning to him or her. We explore how our lives are making a significant impact on one another and the world around us.

Freedom: We openly describe our deepest needs, values, and wishes. We ask that each of these be honored, not judged or adjusted. We state our boundaries and ask that they be respected. We also insist that we do not have to follow standard conventions or male or female stereotypes if we choose not to.

Happiness: We say and show what makes us happy. We want a relationship that includes safety and security, enduring trust, and mutual openness about feelings. We explore each of them and look together for ways to put them in place. We are not afraid to ask for pleasures from our partner, be they sexual or recreational.

Growth: We are committed to caretaking, tending our relationship. We want both of us to join in doing the work required for its upkeep. We want to work conflicts out with one another as they arise. We want to address our issues rather than leaving a long wake of resentment after a conflict. We ask that both of us run the risk of stretching ourselves.

Gradually, it becomes easier, less embarrassing, to ask for what we long for. At the same time, we also know that sometimes we ask for more than almost anyone can give. Then our work is to find ways to say yes to the lower-than-desired dividends that the people around us can offer. This is where longing intersects with reality and we say yes to what is as it is and to others as they are. We have made the transition from longing as an extravagant demand on others to longing as a reasonable request of them: "Gimme what I want right now" becomes "Here I am with my heart opening to show what I want. If it comes my way, I rejoice. If not, I remain open to you. In both instances I remain aware of how what I really want is also in me." We can still have far-fetched longings, but we do not insist that others meet them in the ways we have imagined. As Henry David Thoreau says in *Walden*, "If you have built castles in the air, your work need not be lost; that is where they should be." He adds, however, "Now put the foundations under them." We build our castles on our own; the foundations are built in partnership.

Here are some suggestions that might help us when others fail to meet our longings. First, we can *give* to others what we seek to receive from them. We still focus on finding fulfillment of our longings. But we also focus on how we can help fulfill the longings of others. This will feel like a calling to an elevated form of love. It is rewarding, so we will want to do it more and more:

- We love others as we long to be loved by them.
- We help others find meaning in all that happens to them, but without advising or pushing them to see things our way.
- We abdicate our right to control others, and honor their freedom.
- We do what contributes to the happiness of those around us.

- We want others to evolve and grow rather than continue to need us so much.

Longings seem entirely other-directed. This is because we have always sought their fulfillment outside ourselves. Yet, longings can be self-directed and self-fulfilled in some ways. While remaining open to fulfillment from others we can become unexpected resources to ourselves:

- We love ourselves as we long to be loved by others.
- We look for meaning in all that happens to us.
- We become intent on freeing ourselves from inhibition and compulsion.
- We do what fosters our happiness.
- We find ways to grow from our crises and challenges.

Finally, sometimes we ourselves can't put our finger on which longing is up for us. As a practice, we can explore each of our five longings by asking questions like these:

- Do I feel there is not enough love in my life? Am I yearning for intimacy, and feeling the loss or absence of it? Am I in need of one or more of the five *A*'s?
- Have I lost a sense of meaning in my life, relationship, or work? Do I feel rudderless and purposeless? Am I feeling that what I do has little value?
- Do I feel constricted and restricted? Am I not free to be myself, to do what I want to do, to make the choices that reflect my deepest needs, values, and wishes? Am I the one holding myself back?
- Am I unhappy? Am I depressed, lonely, isolated? Have I lost my lively energy, my joie de vivre? Am I taking everything too seriously? Have I lost my sense of humor? Am I out of touch with my body?

- Am I stuck, not going anywhere, not letting go, not moving forward? Do I find myself in a rut with no hope for a better future? Am I too attached to my safe routine? Have I lost track of my spirituality? Have I given up hope?

> I'm rather surprised. I think it's because, for the first time in my life, I know what I want.
>
> —Joan Fontaine to Cary Grant in the 1941 film *Suspicion*
> (Screenplay by Alma Reville, Joan Harrison, Samson Raphaelson)

Moving toward Fulfillment

> It is not yet clear what we shall become.
> —1 John 3:2

The three qualities of longings—indefinable, enduring, aimed at more than the ordinary—are clues to how to hold our longings. We can do so with serenity rather than with a feverish must-have energy. We can gauge the fulfillment that can come of our longings intelligently and moderately. We can find out who we really are as unique humans. Using our threefold description of longings, we can therefore explore how we hold them placidly, how we move toward a reasonable fulfillment of them, how we come to know more and more of ourselves through them.

Indefinable:

We hold our longings by letting go of having to define, nail down, be exactly sure of what we long for. We can let a longing abide in us with no name. When we do this, we respect our heart's way of knowing and holding.

We move toward fulfillment of our longings by allowing them to fulfill themselves. We give up searching. Instead we trust the universe to grace us with provisional fulfillments little by little. Likewise, we trust that all our longings are in fact at peace, already and always, at a deeply spiritual level within us.

We know ourselves through our longings because in them we see what is truest about us. We enter a realm beyond words, a world of

Hold the space!!.

interiority, the deep-within that is our true self. It is the ego that is adept at defining; our higher life is content with ambiguity and paradox.

Enduring:

We hold our longings by assenting to the fact that a longing can endure for a lifetime. We are in no rush to fulfill any longing. A longing is like pi, the ratio of a diameter to a circumference of a circle. It is a number but has no final ending. We accept the fact that some longings seem charted to remain only longings and not be fulfilled at all. Simply holding them seems to be enough for us.

We move toward fulfillment of our longings when we say yes to the impermanence in any satisfaction. We say yes to not reaching a sense of finality or finding ongoing gratification.

We know ourselves because we come to realize that our identity is about ever-opening rather than finally ending.

The More:

We hold our longings by reaching for what is more than what we have been, more than what we have expected, more than what we thought were our limits. We transcend the boundaries of the ego's world.

We move toward fulfillment when we remain open to what takes us beyond the usual and the ordinary. We find the more that is right here, right now, in all that is around us. Since every longing is for what is ultimately unattainable in any final way, we are always stretching our hearts. We open our hearts in love, meaning, freedom, happiness, and growth, but it is our longings that widen them.

We know ourselves as having a spiritual identity since *spiritual* means "transcendent," that is, the more that we are, the more that we are usually aware of. Our openness to more, our curiosity about more, our yearning for more, are all revelations about just what evolutionary beings we really are.

Regarding knowing ourselves, here are some affirmations we can use daily to maintain our awareness of our longings as a path to enlightened living:

- I cherish the longings I feel for love, meaning, freedom, happiness, growth—ingredients of my humanness.

- I hold each of my longings with serenity rather than craving.
- I appreciate the times I find some fulfillment.
- I let go of believing that anyone or anything can fulfill my longings so completely that they vanish altogether.
- I trust that my longings are fully alive in my higher self, where they reside as the riches of wholeness.
- I choose to live a life of love.
- I make meaningful choices.
- I protect my inner freedom from inhibition, fear, and compulsion.
- I make the choices that lead to happiness for myself and others.
- I see all that happens as an opportunity and summons to evolve.
- May all that I feel and do further our common evolutionary goal: a world of justice, peace, and love.
- May I be ever aware of the precious longing behind every choice I make and have made.

Only by following the inner light of one's own self can the human psyche be comprehended in its fullness.

—HARIDAS CHAUDHURI, *The Concept of Integral Self-Realization*

4

Our Longing for Love

Remember, if you want to make progress on the path and find what you long for, it won't be a matter of thinking much but of loving much. So do whatever best stirs you to love.

—SAINT TERESA OF ÁVILA, *The Interior Castle*

The ancient Greeks spoke of at least four kinds of love: erotic, familial, friendly, and the selfless love that is unconditional and universal. Our longing for love includes all four of these. We long both to give them and to receive them.

EROTIC LOVE: The word *longing* is actually part of the root definition of eros. It is related to the word *erasthai,* which means "longing or desire" in Greek. The Roman version of Eros is Cupid. His name gives us the word *cupidity,* which also implies desire, in this instance, with the connotation of greed. Since such desire is without surcease or a sense of surfeit, it is related to longing.

Erotic love begins in attraction and romance. Romantic love promises fulfillment, an end to our longing. In fact, our longings increase in romance. Yet, we imagine or expect perfect happiness. We see this very illusion in Shakespeare's *The Taming of the Shrew:*

> Happily I have arrived at the last.
> Unto the wished haven of my bliss.

The familiar phrase "happily ever after" does not usually apply to long-term intimate relationships. Many conflicts arise; real love is tested again and again. But relationships can certainly thrive when each disruption of serenity is remedied with sturdy agreements and stable commitments.

Eros is associated with desire for sexual connection, sometimes within a relationship, sometimes outside it. Yet, more is going on than sexual desire. We may actually be longing for affection. A deep longing for oneness may be hidden in a desire for sex. Indeed, the best sex happens when we no longer notice there are two of us. The dualism of desire for something has faded into unitive consciousness, the realm longings lead us into. This is where the tigers of frenzied desire have melted into the butter of authentic fulfillment.

FAMILY LOVE: Some of us want as little contact with our families as possible. Some of us want more contact than we now have or have ever had. But all of us want the warmth of full inclusion in a circle of caring love. That inclination is innate, and family connection is a natural way our yearning is fulfilled. We long to be held in love with all the five *A*'s by those to whom we are physically related. Whether we want the company of family members or not, nothing can erase the family orientation in our human nature. In some cultures that energy extends to a whole village. Nowadays, many of us are learning to form families of friends, and that helps us create a container for familial love. On the humorous side, families also help us discover our level of enlightenment. Time spent with family is guaranteed to show us how far we are from it!

FRIENDSHIP LOVE: True friendship is a form of love that is unconditional. We long for companions who walk beside us, who support us in our crises, who cheer our successes, who hold us in our defeats. We want to know someone is with us in the valley of the shadow of death. When this longing is fulfilled and then suddenly ends, a posttraumatic stress disorder may result. Returning soldiers from Afghanistan say they miss the brotherhood and the sense of purpose they felt so reliably in their combat missions. These are the inveterate longings of the heart for friendly-brotherly love.

UNCONDITIONAL AND UNIVERSAL LOVE: In our evolutionary core, we long to have a heart big enough to include all beings. Such unconditional and universal love practiced by more and more of us grants our planet its only chance to survive. This kind of love connection is collective, a commitment to cosmic welfare, all people our loved neighbors. We can sometimes find a mystical sense of unity consciousness in the depths of ourselves, that is, in our true nature beyond ego. We then experience our oneness with all beings. This is a way to realize that our longing for love as connection is already fulfilled.

At the same time, we might imagine that our longing for love is about needing others and especially needing someone special to love us. In reality, our longing for love, as is true for any longing, can be self-fulfilled in some way too. This applies to all five longings:

Our longing for love can be at least partially satisfied by our love of ourselves, as we continually nurture ourselves with the five *A*'s: attention, acceptance, appreciation, affection, allowing.

Our longing for meaning is fulfilled not only by finding meanings but by making them too. We give meaning to our experiences and relationships when we treat them with respect and honor the sacredness in all that happens and all that is. Sacredness is spiritual meaning.

Our longing for freedom is not only a yearning that others give us space to be ourselves and not control us. We can handle that intrusion the more we act in ways that show others that we are free to be who we really are—and will stand up for that right.

We long for happiness, but we can do what makes us happy, not simply wait for others to help that happen. We can choose a lifestyle that reflects our deepest needs and wishes. We can see our relationships as about happiness, not about the enduring of pain.

Our longing for growth is almost entirely a matter of self-activation. We satisfy our need to grow as we take advantage of every opportunity to do so. Opportunities come our way from life and relationships on a daily basis. They are examples of synchronicity, the meaningful coincidence of many energies that invite us to make the most of the world's many challenges.

What Happens in Relationships

Bats make their way in the dark by listening to the sound of their own voices bouncing off the surfaces around them. This is a metaphor from nature about our viewing one another through our own projections: What we hear is an echo from a voice within ourselves; what we see is a mirror reflection of our own beliefs and feelings about others. We can understand why it is so hard to perceive someone as he or she really is. We do "get" one another authentically, but only in moments, the moments in which projections recede and the real other appears. This won't happen when we merge with someone or when we look *at* her. We find one another when we both enter the space between us. In that Buddha space, the meeting of our mutually enlightened selves, is an ongoing flow of love, meaning, freedom, happiness, growth—the ingredients of true human identity. Sitting together or holding one another in mindful moments with no agenda helps us get there.

What do we actually long for from a partner? In relationships we may be longing for the holding environment of the five *A*'s. We might still be searching for what we needed in childhood and we transfer our original longing for holding on to a partner. This is a normal process, but it is important to our growth to make it conscious and explore it together with our partner. When it is a subtext in our communications, we shuffle between unstated expectations and bewildered reactions.

The longing in any of us to feel loved and cared about, whether that longing is spoken or unspoken, is a longing for a combination of all five *A*'s: attention, acceptance, appreciation, affection, allowing. Intimacy in adult life is connection, nothing less than the five *A*'s being mutually expressed. The five *A*'s are the original needs we had in infancy. They endure in our hearts as longings all our lives. A glance at the origin of the words helps us understand what longing for these *A*'s is really about:

Attention is from the Latin *attendere*, meaning "to stretch toward or reach out." Attention happens when people stretch or reach beyond themselves to focus on us in an engaged, truly interested way. The attentive person is not so absorbed in himself that he cannot see us in our coat of many colors. True attention is meant to be directed to our feelings, words, moods, actions, and needs in all their uniqueness. *A person who loves us will certainly also want to know our every longing.* In addition, true attention is not intrusive, as in scrutiny, but respectful of our boundaries.

In attention we stretch *from ourselves to others. Acceptance* is from Latin *accipere*, meaning "to take something to ourselves." We are accepted by someone when she takes us as we are. In acceptance we are being unconditionally welcomed as adequate, suitable, lovable by the other. Acceptance is the opposite of judgment and rejection. We are never ashamed of who we are. We know that all that we are *belongs*.

Appreciation is from Latin *appretiare*, meaning "to set a price, to place a value on something." We are appreciated when we are valued, when we matter to someone, when we mean something, when our life and well-being are cherished. Our partner has an abiding sense of our worth. Likewise, appreciation of us means that our partner shows us gratitude for what we contribute to the relationship. We are thereby being given recognition, not taken for granted.

Affection is from the medieval Latin word *affectionatus*, meaning "devoted." We feel affection coming our way when people are dedicated to our happiness. We receive affection in psychological and physical ways. Our boundaries are honored in both instances. We feel a warmth and caring in the touch of someone. We do not feel that something is being taken from us in those moments but rather given to us. Affection, like all the five *A*'s, is a gift after all. In healthy relationships, we notice that intimate touching does not have to lead to sex. Though sex is of course included when it is appropriate.

Allowing is from Middle English and old French *alouer,* meaning "to assign as a right." The Latin root is in the word *allocare,* meaning "to place," as in "allocate." We thus have been allocated, as humans, the right to make choices that reflect our own deepest needs, values, and wishes. Allowing is the opposite of controlling. Each of us is free, so it seems that allowing is unnecessary, but in a relationship this *A* refers to being with a partner who respects our uniqueness rather than tries to make us over. We don't need permission to be free, but we do feel loved when someone supports our freedom.

We know we love and are loved when the five *A*'s happen consistently and mutually in our relationships. They are the components of authentic connection, belonging, accompaniment, standing by us, supporting us. They are signs of meaningful love, trustworthiness, foundations of commitment. They show us what intimacy really entails. We long and always longed for attention, acceptance, appreciation, affection, allowing. These are the five names of love. *Who is showing up in these ways toward me? Am I showing up in these ways toward those I love? Do I show up in these ways toward myself?*

We also know we are loved by someone when he or she wants us to find fulfillment for our five longings and does what it takes for that to happen. Likewise, we know that we really love someone when we want to see him or her find fulfillment of the five longings and we foster a relationship that provides them. To love is to want the other to have a meaningful life, to be free and happy, to grow into his or her full human stature.

Most of us are insecure about our lovability. Perhaps our insecurity is a way of nudging us from isolation so we will seek contact with others. Then love and intimate relationship can happen. Likewise, from the opposite viewpoint, perhaps an experience of abandonment might move us to find the beauty of solitude, at least for a time. We are whole when we have no fear about being close or about being alone, when we are open to connection and are safeguarding our aloneness.

Yet, in any case, the fulfillment of our longing for love is complex. What we want from the other is accessible but not fully so. We can only find some fulfillment of the five *A*'s from a partner, not total fulfillment. In a healthy relationship, we will, nonetheless, have many *moments* of fulfillment of the five longings. In those moments, we can feel an inflow of oxytocin, the hormone of relatedness. Then all five *A*'s feel perfectly fulfilled: We feel true belonging because we have contacted one another's essence. We know our bond is meaningful. We are free to be ourselves. We are happy. At the same time, we meet up with growth challenges, but we address them cooperatively. When the five longings meet the five *A*'s, we know what fulfillment really is. It trumps all the promises we have been making, keeping, or breaking.

> Yet, wooing thee, I found thee of more value
> Than stamps in gold or sums in sealed bags;
> And 'tis the very riches of thyself
> That now I aim at.
> —SHAKESPEARE, *The Merry Wives of Windsor*

Tending Our Relationships

Plato pictured our planet as looking like what we might envision today as a soccer ball. The psyche, too, looks like a soccer ball. It is not smooth like a bowling ball. It contains a patchwork of sectors carefully sewn together from childhood onward: our intellect, our emotions, our ego, our body, our dark side, our sexuality, our relationships, our spirituality—to name a few. In the soccer ball of human wholeness each sector requires attention. Each requires its own form of tending, just as each child in a family requires a unique style of caretaking. No one child is meant to be given all the attention; each deserves equal caring. When any one patch of our psyche is ten times bigger than the others, as happens in an addiction, we lose sight of our wholeness. For instance, I realized after the dust settled from my divorce how much of my mental space had been taken up with our drama. Once I was no longer obsessed with my wife/marriage/divorce story, I felt free space opening within me. So much of my psychic territory had been colonized by uproar and ego—I realize, now, by my own choosing. The drama was the third presence throughout the relationship and in its ending. It took quite a while for me to cede that psychic territory back to myself. *Has this happened for you? Do you have and cherish each of the united states of your psyche? Are you fulfilling your role as secretary of the interior, caringly tending each state? We won't forget that little Rhode Island deserves just as much attention as vast Alaska, and has its own unique ecological requirements too.*

Likewise, a longing to experience or maintain love in an intimate relationship places some requirements on how we see one another's longings. This means paying attention to the fact that men and women differ in how they feel longings. Freud admitted that he was stumped by the question "What do women want?" Perhaps he missed the distinction between longing and desiring. Women are more apt to long, to feel what is not easy to put into words or to ask for in any specific way, or to be uncertain about whether a longing is actually fulfilled. Men are more apt to express want or desire and to know definitely whether they are being fulfilled. Men might be uncomfortable with longings because they are too elusive. Likewise, for us men to admit we have longings requires vulnerability, showing a need for others that may be too big an admission for the ego of a "manly guy." For instance, some of us might more easily speak of attraction to a part of the body than to the warm feeling in someone's company. In fact, I have rarely heard men even use the word *longing*. To many men that word sounds sentimental or "too feminine."

To men, women may seem unsatisfiable. Many men may not understand what a woman is asking of them or how to satisfy her needs in a relationship. But this is not a communication issue. It is the very nature of longings to be mostly inexpressible, not known fully even to the one who longs, not finally satisfied even when they are somewhat or abundantly fulfilled. So the question for men is not

"What do women want?" but "How can I appreciate and remain open to a woman's longings—even when neither of us fully understands them?" We also keep in mind that this distinction applies to male-male or female-female relationships too. Freud's better question might have been, "What do deeply sensitive people long for?"

That question places our emphasis on both our self- and other-concerns:

- Safety and security set the scene for the experience of love between people. To protect and expand our longing for love, it is crucial to foster and stay only in relationships that provide safety and security. As soon as we see that it is not safe in the room with a partner, we speak up about it. If we can't be heard, we can't trust that our relationship has a future. We have raised our criterion for relating.

- We are not satisfied only with the physical presence of someone. We stay only with those with whom we feel safely held. Trust is now the key to our remaining in a relationship.

- The experiences of comfort or support from a partner become teaching moments for self-nurturance. *Everyone who loves me as I want to be loved is modeling for me how I can love myself.* This includes realizing that every memory of how a family member came through for me in childhood can now be looked back upon as modeling how to engage in self-care.

- Relationships work best when they combine close connection with respect for differences. A continual integration of union and diversity ensures that our longing for love is in the best position for it to evolve.

- We remain aware of our neediness. What may feel like the deepest intimacy ever is happening in a relationship, but we may really be meeting up with our own neediness as it clings to the promise of satiation. We notice that our sensation is that of a fix rather than a connection. We are caught in adrenaline-rich drama. We take care of ourselves in a relationship when

the hormone of connection, oxytocin, has become more
valuable to us than dopamine, adrenaline, or testosterone.

- This is the statement we say and hear, verbally and
  nonverbally, every minute of every day: "I welcome all that you
  are and offer all that I am."
- We don't make choices that might destabilize the relationship.
  We make the choices that honor, protect, and maintain it.
- We have a new set of criteria for what constitutes a good
  partner or appropriate candidate for a relationship. We see the
  qualities in all the five longings in him or her: She is loving,
  leads a meaningful life, is a free soul, is generally happy, and is
  continually evolving.
- Each partner has become and will remain the protector of the
  bond rather than the defender of his or her own ego.

We can further explore the list above by looking at how we might
be focusing on defending our own ego; such defense is the opposite
of tending a relationship. Maintaining "big ego," that is egotism,
means that we are self-centered, arrogant, controlling, retaliatory,
and believe ourselves entitled to have all our expectations met with
no obligation to reciprocate. An egotist suffers from four compulsions that cancel the maintenance of closeness:

1. He can't apologize because with his mind-set of being right he
   can't admit he was wrong when it is appropriate to do so. He
   can't *take back* what he said.
2. He can't forgive because he has to *get back at* those who hurt
   him.
3. He can't give freely because he has to *get back from* those to
   whom he has given something: "You owe me a favor."
4. He does not have to say "Thank you" because he is entitled
   to *get* all you give him.

"Can't say 'Sorry,'" "can't forgive," "can't give," and "can't
thank" are equivalent to "can't love."

This ego–mind-set of fictions, fears, and self-deceptions is deeply entrenched. It gets in the way of our responding positively to the five longings a partner brings to a relationship with us. We cannot love when egotism prevents us from being truly vulnerable or generously giving. We are not able to see meaning in anything or anyone beyond their usefulness to our needs. We cannot be free because the elements of egotism are all compulsions. We cannot be happy since we are always on guard and notice that people don't like us very much. With egotism in place, we fail to grow because we are "stuck in ego"—Joseph Campbell's definition of hell, solitary confinement.

In the first half of life, most of us are highly ego invested. Then, in the second half of life, that style might be challenged. For instance, we might fail at something, lose our ego-built power in a big way, lose control or status. We then find ourselves facing the experience of powerlessness. We are being called upon to adopt a more realistic and humble way of living—one that will be less stressful too. The unhealthy option is to dig our heels in: "I deserve or need a privileged power position over others, so I will get it back in any way I can." We say no to a level playing field, one that invites partnership. We insist on endorsing our prerogative of power-over. This is another way that egotism cancels intimacy. It can also be a way to let intimacy with someone come into our lives slowly, because too much too soon might be difficult for us.

We can let go of ego and place our psyche under new management, that of our higher, gentler self. Here are some suggestions for how to do so. This list of practices is based on my book *You Are Not What You Think: The Egoless Path to Self-Esteem and Generous Love* (Shambhala, 2015), which explores letting go of egotism in detail:

- Follow the Golden Rule: Act toward others as you would want them to act toward you.
- Keep the needs of others in mind, especially in little ways—an antidote to selfishness.

- Find ways to maintain healthy self-esteem without showing off. It's OK to be a big shot, just don't act that way.
- Let go of ranking, especially of elitism, seeing yourself as above others.
- Acknowledge not knowing something or showing that you need support or help.
- Take feedback as useful information, not as criticism, even when it is meant that way.
- Apologize when you know you have harmed or offended anyone. Make amends if necessary.
- Let go of attempts to control, dominate, or manipulate others.
- Give people leeway and make allowances for their errors rather than pointing out every little thing they do that irks you.
- Welcome disagreement, because it can lead to dialogue. This puts the emphasis in a discussion on arriving at common ground or learning a new truth rather than proving yourself right.
- Cooperate rather than compete; collaborate rather than have to show that you know best.
- In a group, give up having to take center stage.
- Trade in your own ego investment for the good of all concerned or for the accomplishment of the group goal.
- Reconcile yourself to not always getting your way.
- Work conflicts out with people, when they are ready and willing to do so, rather than be resentful, pout, snub, or use the silent treatment—all forms of retaliation.
- Don't hold a grudge against those who wrong you, even when they won't admit it—and stop telling the story of how they offended you. Look for ways to reconcile rather than retaliate.
- Remain on high alert for the entry of your reactive ego: the moment when you take what happened personally, become indignant, interpret an action by someone as a slight to your dignity.
- When someone's ego is aroused toward you, do not dig your heels in or go nose to nose. Simply pause with compassion

toward the pain in his/her ego-reaction and treat it with loving-kindness, while nonetheless not putting up with any abuse.

- In intimate bonds, give up vindicating yourself in order to gratify your ego and instead, let go of your ego to gratify the relationship. Become the protector of the partnership rather than the defender of your own ego.
- Do good to those who hate you, pray for or wish enlightenment for those who have betrayed, failed, or mistreated you.
- See losing face (and all these suggestions) as welcome opportunities for growth in humility, a virtue that makes you more lovable.
- Discard the Ace (arrogance, control, entitlement) of Ego for the Ace of Hearts.

Even with all our limitations, gestures of generosity, solidarity, and caring cannot but well up within us, since we are made for love.

—POPE FRANCIS, *Laudato si'*

5

Our Longing for Meaning

Being human always points, and is directed to something or someone, other than oneself—be it a meaning to fulfill or another human being to encounter. The more one forgets himself—by giving himself to a cause to serve or to another person to love—the more human he is.

—Viktor Frankl, *Man's Search for Meaning*

The word *meaning* refers most simply to the definition of a word or a symbol. *Meaning* also refers to "importance," that is, "significance or impact." *Meaningful* refers to a depth in the level at which we cognitively understand and bodily experience something.

We say our life is meaningful when it makes a difference, has a purpose, yields personal fulfillment. We feel our life is meaningful when we are committed to something greater than ourselves, when we believe we have a place in the world, when we feel that we are here for a reason, that our life matters, that we matter. This happens most felicitously when we love what we do, when we are enjoying the beauty of something, making a contribution to others, dedicating ourselves to a cause. We can now understand why Viktor Frankl, in the quotation above, sees a link between meaning and a loving life purpose. Deep meaning is certainly visible in great love. For

68

instance, here is an epitaph in a nineteenth-century graveyard in New England that I have never forgotten:

Annie, 9 years old, a life of love.

Little Annie fulfilled the longing for meaning in herself and others—and for me when I was so touched by her epitaph. I carry Annie's epitaph in my memory and it makes *my* life more meaningful. Memories held in the locket that is our heart have that power for all of us.

Meaning is also used in the sense of "meant for." This refers to what something is intended for; for example, a safe is meant for storing valuables. Metaphorically, we might say, "The human heart was meant for love." In both instances, *meant for* is a way of pointing to the design and destiny of something, its ultimate purpose, the why of it. To long for meaning makes us spelunkers in these intriguing hollows of human life.

According to a recent Gallup poll, sixty percent of Americans describe themselves as happy and not overwhelmed by anxiety. Yet, according to the Centers for Disease Control, forty percent either do not feel that their lives have a meaningful purpose or are neutral about it. A sense of purpose and meaning increases feelings of well-being. When the main drive in life is only our own gratification, we are less likely to find well-being. The irony is that being happy in a reliably ongoing way is directly proportional to a life that is animated by a sense of giving and of service to others. When we live that way, we have transcended ourselves because we are being moved by a wider concern than our immediate satisfactions. Happiness is immediate but passing. Purpose is not always immediate, but it is lasting. We see again that each longing is hitched to all the others.

One of the most wonderful qualities in us is our capacity to find meaning in any conditions or circumstances. Indeed, we are the custodians of meaning. When bad things happen to us, we are more apt to find a meaning or useful lesson in our suffering that has been, until then, unnoticed. Likewise, people with a sense of purpose and meaning automatically intensify their connection to others who suffer as they do. Compassion results, the response of love to others' pain. When personal pleasure is our only goal, our world is small; when an evolutionary purpose drives us, our world inflates to its authentic bigness.

Finding meaning also has a cellular component. The brain naturally tries to organize data, no matter how random, into intelligible concepts, meaningful patterns, or coherent concepts. This may be why we sometimes see figures in clouds, a face in the moon. Such an orientation toward meaning is physical because it enlists brain cells. Likewise we feel a physical sensation of relief or satisfaction when we find order in what was unintelligible before. We also notice a physical reaction that shows us what something means to us. Our response can be aesthetic, erotic, suspenseful, attractive, repulsive, absorbing, disturbing. We might feel a lump in our throat, a constriction in our chest, an opening in our heart area. These are telltale signs of meaning. Our bodily experience might show us a meaning that our mind can't fathom or define. This is a here-and-now experience without projections and judgments, the very definition of mindfulness. Such mindful awareness is thus a way of contacting meaning. We are seeing something as it is. This allows its significance to come through. Our body keeps joining in on our longings, as it does on anything of importance.

Projecting Too Much Meaning

We notice that some things have only the level of meaning that their outward appearance indicates. For instance, the meaning of a stop sign is "Stop!" If the sight of a stop sign arouses us to rebellion, we have surely added a meaning that was not meant to be there. This enlarging of meaning regularly happens in an addiction. In fact, giving something a larger meaning than fits the bill can be seen as a sign of addiction. For instance, food is meant to be fuel and enjoyment. When we add meanings like control, escape from boredom, filling our inner emptiness, giving ourselves comfort, recalling the safety of childhood, we are adding meanings that can lead to a misuse of food. Likewise, alcohol is meant for social fun, but when we add a meaning like escape from feelings, we are using it for more than what constitutes social drinking, its healthy purpose. Little Johnny Walker is now walking all over us. Sex means love and mutuality, but when we use it to boost our ego or as a weapon, it takes on meanings that cancel intimacy, the wonderful meaning it could have had.

There is a literary device called "pathetic fallacy." This refers to assigning a bigness or importance to something or someone when it is not warranted. We engage in this fallacy when we "add value" to certain people, things, and events in our lives. We let a man or woman become so important that our happiness depends on whether he or she likes or approves of us. Giving people that bigness is making them into a higher power. We are then seeking the unlimited, God, in a person, limited. "I can only be satisfied if I have that woman or man" makes the meaning of satisfaction too restricted. We are actually giving our power to someone and then seeing it in him. The bigness he or she has in our psyche is our own power looking back at us. Bigness is a mirror image. Grounded assessment of people and things, on the other hand, is based on observation, not on projection. We neither idealize nor demonize, only humanize.

Another element of "meaning" is personal significance. We say affectionately, "You mean a lot to me." We are saying that someone does a lot to fulfill our longing both for meaning and for love. However, projection can rear its head here too. People imagine qualities and meanings in one another that may not match the reality of who they are. For instance, someone can seem to be all we ever wanted but prove eventually to be just what we did not want at all. Likewise, we sometimes wonder why people act toward us as they do. They might be basing their approach to us on their version of what we mean to them. For instance, someone might see us as a father or mother figure, as a model, an erotic object, a source of comfort, a threat, a villain, a reflection of the worst part of himself. This subjective sense of who we are may lead them to have very specific expectations of us, beliefs about us, biases toward us, likes or dislikes of us. What creates problems in our relationships is carrying expectations of one another that we have not mutually agreed upon. In healthy relating, we check out one another's meanings and align them with reality—a major, and sometimes lifelong, task.

Our strong reactions to others can signal to us that we are investing some words or actions with a bigger meaning than is appropriate to the circumstance. Here is an example: We were criticized and judged in childhood by one or both of our parents. Because of that experience, criticism has become bigger to us than the extent of its definition in the dictionary. Our psychological work as adults is to see how many concepts have become inflated or deformed by our past experience and turned into projections. The work is grieving the past and letting go of it. Then, such experiences as being criticized in the present as we were in the past become bite-size and fully digestible en route to excretion. Indeed, to know that the past influences us is to have begun to free ourselves from it. Likewise, to be aware of our limitations is already to have begun transcending them.

In our relationships, we want the meaning of what we say or feel to be "heard" by others. We also want to be able to trust that our needs and their importance, that is, their meaningfulness, are respected. This is all part of the *A* of attention in the five *A*'s. Such a desire to be understood makes sense and is a legitimate goal in any trusting relationship. However, we might also want to consider another option, one that can make life easier for us and those around us: As we age, we don't need as much attention as we did in the past. It is no longer such a big deal to be "heard" accurately every time, to have our needs understood and fulfilled in a "just right" way. Being heard like that some, or occasionally none, of the time has become good enough for us. As full-on adults our focus is less and less on how others attune to us, take to us, or take care of us. Our focus moves to how we can do this for ourselves. "Do I give myself all five of the *A*'s?" As we learn to self-soothe, we ask for less from partners or friends. In fact, this shift shows us we are becoming adults. We still want the five *A*'s from others. We continue to appreciate those who do hear us and do respond to us. But we don't need them so badly that our serenity is seriously ransacked when they aren't forthcoming from those around us. Regarding self-soothing, we recall the aspiration of Saint Madeleine Sophie Barat, founder of the Society of the Sacred Heart, for "a gentle heart that holds and calms its own anxieties."

With every passing year as we evolve into adulthood, we notice two changes in ourselves: We have said yes to the given that sometimes we will be heard and sometimes not, that not everyone will attend to our needs every time. We are not resentful toward them for their deficiency. We don't blame them for what they don't or can't give.

Secondly, we make up for what others fail at by being more and more self-nurturant. In other words, we do what we started to do in childhood—we take over, one by one, the functions our parents fulfilled for us. We are meant to keep doing that all our lives. The word *meant* in the preceding sentence refers to the fact that our life has adult meaning because we are accepting others' limitations with a combination of a kindly shrug and an ever-renewed self-care.

This program of behavior makes sense in a relationship in which the word *sometimes* is appropriate. But if a partner just about never hears us, just about never responds to our needs, then we face a new challenge. Now our option is not the shrug but therapy that can help the relationship improve for both of us. We do not put up with no or minimal nonfulfillment of needs nor with abuse. We take action for change or else we move on.

On a humorous note, we might imagine a new job title: not body-guard but heart-guard. Many of us would have benefited from having a guardian by our side who intervened to shield our tender hearts when our parents or others were pummeling them. Becoming a strong, self-nurturant adult means being our own heart-guard. When someone crosses our boundaries now, we can say, "No, stand down, I won't be treated that way. I am protecting my vulnerable heart from insult, criticism, betrayal, abuse."

The Ever-Unfolding Yarn

> We are all faced throughout our lives with agonizing deci-
> sions, moral choices. Some are on a grand scale. Most of
> these choices are on lesser points. But we define ourselves
> by the choices we have made. We are in fact the sum
> total of our choices. Events unfold so unpredictably, so
> unfairly, human happiness does not seem to have been
> included in the design of creation. It is only we, with
> our capacity to love, that give meaning to the indifferent
> universe. And yet, most human beings seem to have the
> ability to keep trying and even to find joy from simple
> things like their family, their work, and from the hope
> that future generations might understand more.
>
> —WOODY ALLEN, *Crimes and Misdemeanors*

Is our life simply a series of events, or is it a coherent story unfolding
with a meaning and purpose? We can begin with the question "What
is the difference between a story and a life line?" A story has a story
line, with a design shaped by the author. A story has a plot, a series
of events that happen by cause and effect, chance, synchronicity, or
contrivance. The story will have continuity, make sense, follow an
arc to a completion. The purpose of the story will be clear by the
time the story ends.

A life line differs from a story in that it can move from event to
event with no particular shape or coherence. People come and go,
predicaments arise, feelings happen, but they do not necessarily
coalesce into a clear story line. Our life can be inchoate, without
direction, even seeming inconsequential to us or others. It will be
up to us to create a bricolage from all the strands of our experiences,
however disparate. We can challenge ourselves to construct a coherent story as we look back at what has happened to us. Every character and event then contributes to the emerging meaning and moves
in the direction of denouement and resolution.

It will be up to us to see a plotline in our life so far. The story waiting to be told in all humans is that of a heroic journey. The model of this story is the following: departure from what has become routine, empty, or aimless; entry into a struggle to reach a useful goal; and then return to where the story began, but with gifts, the main one being more fulfillment than before of the five longings. The hero or heroine finds ways to share his or her gifts, always appreciating the dimension of grace in them. We see meaning in our own lives when we ask where we find ourselves now in these phases of a heroic journey.

We sometimes imagine that our life would have been more meaningful if we had made other choices or if different things had happened to us. Yet, meaning does not depend on just this choice or just this happening. Meaning is protean; it fits itself into any circumstance. We can design a meaningful life out of any choice we have made. In Buddhism, the enlightened way begins from anywhere. We see this also in Isaiah 30:21: "Whether you turn to the right or to the left, your ears will hear a voice behind you, saying, 'This is the way; walk in it.'" No matter what our story has been, we are still able to find a meaning in it. If our life had proceeded in an entirely different direction than the one it took, we would still see meaning in it now as we look back. The wonderful thing about meaning is its promiscuity; it goes with and embraces anyone and anything.

In the course of life many unexpected and meaningful coincidences occur that point to or move us along on our journey. The point of synchronicity is that every life can be a story with an arc of meaning we can follow.

Here is a practice that can encourage that to happen: In your journal, write about each decade of your life. If you were born, for instance, in 1963, begin with the 1960s and move to the 2010s. Treat this part of the exercise as if your life were a play. First list the cast of characters in that decade, each with a description of his or her role—for example, teacher, mother, and so forth—then the locations, then the events that happened with no commentary, just headlines.

Now, look carefully for a thread of similar themes that show what you were up to, and what seemed to be the coherent meaning in all that happened to you. Find a purpose in that decade. It can be how you found a relationship, how you grew into a person of integrity, how you kept gaining and showing more love, advanced in a career, parented, committed to a cause, found yourself either thriving or just surviving. You might note how the characters and events contributed or failed to contribute to the achievement of your stated goal. Finally, track each of the five longings to see how they were fulfilled in each decade.

You may want to continue using this model: Read what you have written and match your life events and its characters to what Aristotle said in his *Poetics:* The plot of a play has to have events that relate to each other as necessary or probable. In addition, the plot has to arouse feelings, such as pity and fear. A character in a drama has three options: He can know what has to be done and do it. He can know and fail to do it. He can know and do it but be ignorant of the implications of what he did. The tragic flaw is in the miscalculation or wrong choice that leads to a downfall.

Now add three more options to Aristotle's list and apply them to yourself: A character might not know what has to be done and not do it. He might not know and stumble into knowing and do it. He might not know, stumble into knowing, and not follow through to do it. This third option is the tragedy of an unfulfilled lifetime. Sometimes we know and don't know at the same time. Such a quandary might be accompanied by frustrated or futile attempts to reach for what we have never guessed we truly deserved. Perhaps we gave up hoping we could ever see the gold ribbon around a neck like ours.

Here is an alternative exercise: We can look at our life as a novel. We can see how the characters, events, motivations, and choices in our lives fit into the bell-shaped curve of a good story:

1. Beginning at Baseline: The story begins with an introduction to the characters and the circumstances they are in.

2. Rising up the Curve: A conflict or crisis occurs that arouses reactions, builds tensions, increases suspense.
3. Crest of the Curve: The climax is the height of the tension, the turning point of the tale. It occurs often because of a decision or action of the protagonist, who is now engaging fully in a conflict. An example is contending with enemies who are trying to keep him from reaching his goal.
4. Sliding down the Curve: The tensions are lessening as things begin to pull together, but there are still questions and not yet a satisfactory conclusion.
5. Ending: A denouement occurs with a resolution of conflicts, an end to suspense, a sense of completion, and a new horizon lining up for a sequel.

How do these five elements fit for your story? What is the status of the five longings in each of the phases?

Look over all you have written and look into what you have learned from this exercise. The significant events in your life probably feel like a combination of choice and inevitability. Ask yourself how much of each important event in your life was your choice and how much seem fated to be. You will then notice the synchronicities that stitch your life together and weave it into a whole.

Give a name to your story, a name to each chapter. Write a commentary on your story as if you were doing a book report. Look all this over and see if you can detect a design in it that is spiritually oriented. What spiritual power has been trying to come through? How has what happened made you more or less spiritually conscious? Which events and characters contributed to your spiritual growth? Ask, "Why have I been here?" There is no final or universally satisfying answer to this or to any of life's riddles, but they do prompt questions that help us know ourselves: "What graces have been given to me?" "What can I give myself to?" "What is the question the universe asked when I was born and to which I am the only answer?"

Finally, ask yourself this question: "Will my life have a surprise ending?"

> There are many trails in this life but the one that matters most few . . . are able to walk. . . . It is the trail of a true human being. I think you are on this trail. It is a good thing for me to see. It is good for my heart.
> —MICHAEL BLAKE, *Dances with Wolves*

Our Interior Framework

> The urge to wander that has made me so restless for the greater part of my life . . .and lures me again and again into all manner of hazards and encounters, does not stem so much from a thirst for adventure as from a longing to find my own restful place in the world—to arrive at a point where I could correlate all that might happen to me with all that I might think and feel and desire.
> —MUHAMMAD ASAD, *The Road to Mecca*

A framework is a structure that holds something together and supports it. A framework, understood philosophically, is whatever helps us make sense of—find meaning in—ourselves, the world, our choices. A framework is whatever we keep coming back to when we need to make sense of what we are and do in the face of what happens to us. Our personal framework correlates—as Asad, the influential and visionary European Jewish-born Muslim scholar, says above—and integrates all that happens and has happened into a lucid and coherent whole. Our framework can't be fixed and dogmatic since our inner instinct is to go on a journey, to be ever moving, continually unfolding. We can't have a framework that is imprisoning and stultifying.

Some people do not challenge themselves to invent their own framework. They are content to embrace the one handed to them by family, society, or religion and then to stay put in it. Others take what works from their heritage and discard what seems inappropriate. Some people choose to reject their heritage altogether and develop their own totally alternative framework. This last option is hard to imagine. Something from our past is always in our present, though we may not know it.

In the past, and for many people now, religion served and serves as a trusty framework, one that gives us structure and an ethical stance. When religion becomes dogmatic and does not move with the times, we might change our framework to something we more often now refer to as spirituality, a kind of religion that is personally designed rather than ready made and handed to us by an institution. People who have a framework, such as a spiritual program, that keeps evolving seem to do better with satisfying their unique longing for meaning.

With a well-designed, lively framework, we have a containing border around our story, a clear outlook on the world, an integrated configuration of what life is about. Then we more easily know our place in it. We have a personally created context in which to place our experiences. It is an interior structure that fits for us and integrates all that happens to us. We find safety and contentment in an orderly sense of the whole. With no framework, we feel "out there," with nothing to fall back on, nothing to turn to. We won't feel that way when we have and trust a framework. This will be especially true when our framework is unique in its construction, containing our own learnings and those of the people we respect. Our framework is a backdrop and an inner holding environment. All we feel, do, and are fits in it comfortably. All that happens enters it with ease. All that has been, is, or will be is compostable in this inner garden.

Here are examples of facing a question both with and without an interior framework. We might ask, "Why are people mean?"

With no framework, or with only ego to go on, we might believe we should be that way too, a dog-eat-dog style.

With the Buddhist interior framework, based on loving-kindness, we see such people as confused and we feel compassion for them.

With the framework of the Sermon on the Mount, we ask, "What practices can help me love my enemies? What graces can I call upon?"

With a Jungian framework, we acknowledge that all of us have a shadow side, including ourselves, and we try to examine our own projections upon others.

With a humanist framework, we might ask this question: "How is life putting me on the spot in the face of this meanness and what response is it asking of me?" We then embrace commitments and choices that help us be humane while not permitting abuse.

With contemporary spirituality as a framework, we say yes to the given of meanness in some people and do what we can to defend ourselves while not retaliating. Our commitment to love serves as a framework that withstands anything that might happen. This kind of dedication is described well by Shakespeare in *Troilus and Cressida:*

> Time, force, and death,
> Do to this body what extremes you can;
> But the strong base and building of my love
> Is as the very center of the earth,
> Drawing all things to it.

I have presented some familiar frameworks. We keep in mind, however, that there are many to choose from. In addition, each of us can form his or her own entirely unique framework.

Our longing for meaning is not only about finding a perspective that makes sense. It is also about its beneficial effect on our behavior. Thus, when we have a framework that is meaningful to us, we can find our bearings in any circumstance and know how to navigate our way through it. Using our original example, we can both understand and respond to the experience of meanness in others. For example, the Buddhist framework does this by making it all an opportunity for the practice of loving-kindness. A Twelve Step recovery-program framework does it by acceptance of what can't be changed, courage to change what can be changed, and the wisdom to know the difference.

Every framework relates directly to how we hold our longings. For instance, in Buddhist teaching the ultimate-unsatisfiability element no longer bothers us so much because our framework has made sense of the limitations in human experience. We see, likewise, that all is transitory and we have chosen a framework that includes an unconditional yes to that given.

We all feel anxiety about endings, changes, incompletions, disappointments, uncertainties. A useful practice is to ask ourselves two questions: "What do I need to let go of?" and "What can I say yes to now?" The first question helps us grieve; the second helps us move on. Indeed, a framework has qualities that support our journeying style. For example, we can thrive on what is incomplete because it keeps us actively moving, imaginatively responding, continually opening. We can handle disappointment because it is a path to enlightenment. We can live with uncertainty, even about all five longings, because it is a passport to creativity.

Finally, we remind ourselves that everyone experiences periods, brief or long, when life seems meaningless. No matter how firm our framework, we all confront the demon of meaninglessness at one time or another. The appropriate response in his menacing presence is simply to sit and take notice. Sometimes the demon stares back at us silently and stolidly, confirming our guess, offering even less. To sit is our way of saying yes, let it be. We simply stay and wait, resisting all attempts to change, fix, or end anything. How ironic that sometimes "no meaning" is where the longing for meaning takes us. We recall World War I poet Alan Seeger: "It may be he shall take my hand and lead me into his dark land." That is not the journey we expected, but it is sometimes the one that awaits us. And we Captains Courageous are up for it.

> Everywhere there are traces of, and a yearning for, a unique support . . . a unique reality in which other realities are brought together in synthesis, as stable and universal as matter, as simple as spirit. . . . Having come face-to-face with a universal and enduring reality to which

one can connect . . . fragmentary moments of happiness
that . . . excite the heart without having to satisfy it . . . a
glorious unsuspected feeling of joy invaded my soul.
—PIERRE TEILHARD DE CHARDIN, *Writings in Time of War*

Appreciating Metaphors

A metaphor is a royal road to meaning. As a comparison, a metaphor
shows us a unity in two dissimilar things. We see a similarity that
surprises us into a deeper sense of a thing or of ourselves. Metaphors
provide a richer way of seeing than is possible from regarding only
the surface of things or when we take things too literally.

In literature a metaphor is an implied comparison, a device that
can use a concrete term to describe what is abstract. For instance,
we say, "He is thin skinned," meaning "He is sensitive." The word
skin is palpable, concrete, while the true meaning, "sensitivity," is
abstract. Since everything around us in the world can describe a
feature of our inner life, everything is a metaphor—one of Goethe's
insights.

Here is a personal example of how awareness of a metaphor
helped me know myself a little better: I was recently looking at rock
sculptures by the bay in San Francisco. They were stacks of rocks
balanced in an artistic way, each one very delicately supporting the
others. I immediately thought to myself: "I wonder how parts of me
are stacked and balanced in my psyche? In what position is personality, childhood, religion, sexuality? What is holding up what?"
These questions led me to ponder and thereby learn more about
myself and my inner life. If I had seen only rocks in piles—the literal
view—I would have found out nothing about myself, nor would I
have been able to share my insight on this page. Notice how art so
easily lends itself to metaphor, perhaps its central power and value
in our lives.

A metaphor is often a comparison between something external
and an internal feeling, attitude, or experience. For instance, Francesca wants to say that her boyfriend, Xavier, is a very gentle person.

She uses a metaphor: "Xavier is such a *pussycat.*" Francesca is comparing Xavier's personality—interior reality—to the qualities in a gentle cat—exterior traits. The more we ponder a metaphor, the more we uncover. For instance, when Francesca says that Xavier is a pussycat, she might also ask herself, "*How* is Xavier a pussycat?" As Francesca keeps exploring, she may find that she is discovering something more than the fact that Xavier is gentle. She may perceive—or *need* Xavier—to be submissive. Yet, cats can turn on us too. Francesca may wonder why she did not think of Xavier as a lamb, which does not turn on us. Perhaps Francesca has a suspicion that Xavier can turn on her someday, or already has. Francesca can now ask herself if she feels safe in the relationship with Xavier; perhaps her sense of safety depends on Xavier not asserting himself. Her conscious ambivalence about her partner may then remind Francesca of her relationship to her father. She may see a transference from father onto Xavier. (This line of inquiry is especially significant since the word *metaphor* is Greek for "transference"!)

In another example, our friend Alice says she is thinking of changing careers. We notice her ambivalence and hear ourselves using a spontaneous metaphor: "Are you on the fence about it?" Alice tells us that is exactly how she feels. We then ask her to describe herself as *literally* on a fence. Alice responds, "I have one foot pointing into one yard and the other pointing into the other yard *but neither foot is on the ground.*" This helps Alice process her dilemma as being about feeling ungrounded or torn between two options. Now we are deepening our sense of the topic because we are no longer talking only about the content: changing careers. The metaphor uncovered a whole new harvest to draw from. By synchronicity, just the right image came along from us to lead Alice into her inner world—as just the right White Rabbit led the other Alice into hers.

Our Alice continues to reflect on how her metaphor applies to her seeking guaranteed security in all circumstances and relationships. Her Buddhist background then helps her realize that actually there is no reliable ground to stand on anywhere. To see that takes a more superior intelligence than ego can muster. It is Alice's true nature, her awakened mind, that can understand and embrace her own groundlessness without fear.

We are seeing how metaphors are ways of fulfilling our longing for meaning. Our longing for meaning is not just about finding the grand significances in philosophy. It is also directed to any insight into what our life and relationships are really about. Here is a relationship example: When our partner says of our relationship, "Recently, it hasn't been as much of an uphill battle as it used to be," we get much more information than just "Things have gotten a little better." We go with the image "uphill battle" and so much more emerges about the difficult nature of the relationship. We might find out a good deal more by asking ourselves, "How has the relationship been like a battle?" In both personal and relationship issues, a metaphor is a rich mine of processing; it is a way of tracking and exploring at the feeling-experiential level. In this instance, we are finding out that, from our partner's point of view, life with us has not been cooperative but oppositional. Now we are understanding the meaning of the relationship to our partner—and something about what love requires too.

We see in these examples that metaphors are improvisational. In art, improvisation is an engaged focus on the immediate moment, which becomes a response. It therefore has a liberating quality. We are suddenly open to and act on what is emergent rather than sticking to what we planned. Likewise, metaphors can come out in our speech spontaneously. Since they are not thought up, not a product of our left brain, they come from a deeper precinct of our psyche than our thinking mind. Metaphors come from our higher self, our symbol-making unconscious, a treasury of meaning-laden images. They have resided in all humans since ancient times. They constitute the source from which dreams are constructed. Therefore, metaphors can give important clues about what is going on in our usually unvisited interior world. This is why metaphors are so connected to our longing for meaning.

Metaphors come from within and take us to the emergent beyond, to a future so far unguessed. In that sense, they are also evolutionary. Rabbi Arthur Green takes up this theme in *Radical Judaism: Rethinking God and Tradition:* "The entire course of evolution . . . proceeding onward into the unknown future . . . [is] a meaningful process. There is a One that is ever revealing itself to us within and behind the great diversity of life. That One is Being itself, the constant in the endlessly changing evolutionary parade."

Metaphors matter also in the world beyond consciousness. We can work with our dreams by taking their images as metaphors. We see tangible things and characters in a dream and they have symbolic significance for our conscious life. They are symbols of parts of ourselves that our unconscious, our inner healer, exhibits to us so we can know ourselves better. The dream image in our psyche is an echo, mirroring what is ready to emerge. Our images are summonses to our future. Our dreams are grace-given responses to our longing for meaning.

Along these lines, many of us have found ourselves consistently drawn to a certain image or reality over the years. This isn't generally something we plan; it simply happens. We are consciously aware of it and might dream of it also at times. The object is something that has captured our imagination, kept us fascinated, been a significant focus no matter how our other interests may have changed. We might have a sense of awe and wonder about, for instance, the sea, statuary, dance, an animal, social consciousness, religion. Our attraction is an example of synchronicity, a meaningful coincidence between an external reality and an inner meaning. The mysterious magnetism of the image is a key to the mystery of ourselves. Anything that has retained such persistent importance for us over the decades is a clue to who we really are, a metaphor for what our destiny can be. The object can be a code for our calling, our journey, our end. It can be a trigger to our awakening. It can be a path to love, meaning, freedom, happiness, or growth. It will follow that the more we pay attention to what has held significance for us over the years, the closer we come to the mystery of our longings and our story. For instance, a woman might have been drawn to the world of art for as long as she can remember. This interest can blossom into her becoming an artist, designer, art teacher. It may also make her a person of unusual sensitivity in the world and in relationships too. She may ultimately find ways to invest her talent in making the world a better place.

Finally, we acknowledge that left-brain thinking has its own depth. We can compare the difference between the depth in ordinary thinking processes and the depth we gain from attention to metaphor. This helps us appreciate the value of both sides of our mental processes. We can look for ways to use these listings as practices in our personal lives and in our relationships:

We Gain Depth in Our Thinking by:	We Gain Depth in Relating to Others by Attention to Metaphor by:
Noticing implications	Hearing what is being communicated at a feeling and archetypal level, what is beneath the words, the connotation beyond the denotation
Raising questions and seeking deeper insight	Exploring what a person means so we can appreciate her authentic needs and wishes
Making associations	Noticing how the present concerns of someone relate to past experiences with us
Evoking transference from the unconscious	Contemplating what happens in a relationship so it can stir up our memories of other relationships or of childhood and the transferences that might be happening in this one
Seeing universal applications	Seeing how what is happening in the moment in the relationship can apply to how we can love all beings

We Gain Depth in Our Thinking by:	*We Gain Depth in Relating to Others by Attention to Metaphor by:*
Taking into account subtle, ordinarily hidden meanings	Being open to another so that the meaning she really wants to communicate, perhaps hidden even from herself, might emerge through our dialogue
Being aware of the abstract rather than the concrete only	Looking past the immediate issue to a larger meaning
Recognizing an alternative to taking things literally	Seeing how this present concern is a metaphor for how the relationship has been proceeding so far
Recognizing far-reaching effects	Being aware of the effects of our present behavior on our relationship and on our future together
Appreciating complexity	Never imagining that an issue is only what it seems but appreciating its complex significance
Acknowledging the ambiguity of events and meanings, how they are not pat and settled but are continually opening in new and innovative ways	Being comfortable with ambiguity and uncertainty rather than insisting everything be totally clear or cleared up right now
Realizing that some realities defy explanation	Remaining aware that love and relationship are ultimately mysterious and letting that be satisfactory and even welcome because we find great appeal in that which is endlessly provocative

6

Our Longing for Freedom

Only by facing experiences directly can we become free
of their domination. In this way, they no longer dictate
who we are.

—Ezra Bayda, *Beyond Happiness*

A longing is always for more than the ordinary. Thus, our longing
for freedom is for wider and more personal liberties than we
have in daily civic life. For instance, we long to be who we really are
beyond what is approved by others. We want to be free of their
power over us, to no longer let them have a say over how we live
our lives.

We long for the freedom to be who we really are in thought,
word, and deed. That does not seem like too much to ask. Yet, in
our attitudes, choices, and lifestyle, we notice many ways in which
it is not happening. So much of what seems to be ourselves has been
inputted into us from our childhood, school, religion, society, or
peers. What in me is actually *I*?

We notice how unsafe we often feel in showing—or even
knowing—the many-splendored thing that is our true self. Deep
within us is an enduring and poignant longing for the courage to be

ourselves in all that we believe, do, feel, and are. Our longing for freedom depends for its fulfillment on our accessing that courage.

Freedom to be ourselves becomes a formidable challenge in some relationships. At times we can be caught in taxing adrenaline-driven dramas with others, especially in intimate relationships or within family. We are only free to be ourselves when we are no longer obsessed, addictively attached, or holding onto expectations of or judgments about others. In fact, precisely what we let go of in mindfulness meditation is what helps us find personal freedom: judgment, fear, craving, blame, shame, or attachment to an outcome. In mindful awareness, we are no longer designing our lives on the basis of what others may have come to mean, do, or be in our minds. The result is the freedom to stand firmly on the earth as who we really are. Our hearts have always longed for that groundedness. Sadly, in emotional turmoil with others it is hard to take notice of what our hearts are asking, let alone say yes.

Freedom cannot be defined as limited to any one state of being. Thus, for instance, freedom is not necessarily found either in independence from others or in closeness to them. Freedom is not synonymous either with commitment or no commitment. Freedom is unconditioned. As a state of being, it can exist in any circumstance. We can be unfree on the street or free in a prison. We see this option described so charmingly in the poem "To Althea, from Prison" by the seventeenth-century poet Richard Lovelace:

> Stone walls do not a prison make,
> Nor iron bars a cage;
> Minds innocent and quiet take
> That for a hermitage.
> If I have freedom in my love,
> And in my soul am free,
> Angels alone, that soar above,
> Enjoy such Liberty.

The phrase "in my soul am free" reminds us that our longing for freedom is about more than a right to do what we want. For instance, we felt we were freer when we no longer lived with our parents. That is basic freedom of choice and movement: "I can do more of what I want." This is quantitative. At a soul level, however, freedom is qualitative: "I can be more of who I am." We desire the freedom to come and go as we please. We long for the freedom to be fully who we are in all our comings and goings.

At the deepest level of our being we long to free ourselves from any inhibition, impediment, or constraint on what it takes for us to open into our full humanity. Thus, our longing for freedom is ultimately a challenge to ourselves. We long for the courage to be free enough to be exactly who we are, ultimately an enterprise in our own hands. What we will turn out to be can't be based on old restrictions or shame-based threats that we once had to obey. We can work on releasing ourselves from them. In therapy this means that we address, process, and resolve the issues that still plague us from our past, grieving the painful part, appreciating the positive part. Eventually, we retain only mental memories with no emotional charge in their wake. That is resolution, letting go, freedom from the past.

Indeed, we are only free when we are no longer blaming anyone for the shape our life has taken. People from our past may still have enormous power over our lives and choices. We can ask, "How much of who I am is still based on who Dad was? Is Dad now a ventriloquist so that my voice, attitudes, beliefs, ways of reacting to people and circumstances are really coming from him? How are my choices conditioned by his demands on me, my imitating or opposing him? When will I be on my own?"

I noticed that what helped me especially was finally coming to a radical, unconditional yes to how my childhood was and then automatically feeling compassion for all the players—including me. Freedom is in that yes. It puts an end to resistance to the givens of life, one of which is that we don't always get what is best for us from others. We are on the road to freedom when we let go of arguing with or complaining about the facts of our past. It helps to realize that all of us are subject to variables. No one of us has a special deal from the universe; no one is exempt from what can happen to anyone. A yes to that fact frees us from ego's illusion of entitlement to immunity. We all sometimes misread, run from, or object to our own reality. We reject our dance partner. Freedom happens best in absolute fealty to reality, no matter how unappealing it may have been or is today. Our attachment to having everything go our way is then loosened. We are no longer seeking ways to outmaneuver or dodge reality. As we move from control to yes, we feel our longing for freedom gradually being fulfilled.

We certainly realize that no one can be totally free, but everyone can become somewhat freer each day. In such slow and steady progress our emphasis is on more and more resilience in the face of challenges. Then nothing that happens or has happened can plunge us into despair, because we trust that there is a strength in us to handle it. Our longing to be set free has become trusting that we can free ourselves.

A slave is one who waits for someone to come and free him.
—EZRA POUND

From Compliance to Choice

> All experience has shown that mankind are more disposed to suffer . . . than to right themselves by abolishing the forms to which they are accustomed. But . . . it is their right, it is their duty, to throw off such government, and to provide new guards for their future security.
>
> —*Declaration of Independence*

Freedom, at its most basic, is the right and ability to make and act on our own choices. The philosopher John Stuart Mill, in *On Liberty*, distinguished two ways of experiencing freedom. First, we are free to act according to our own choices and wishes. Second, we are free when we are not coerced or restrained. Thus, there is a freedom *to* and freedom ~~from.~~ The former is in the certitude that we have the power and agency to act. The latter is in freedom from inhibition, fear, habit, or compulsion—obstacles to freedom. We explore both these options in this chapter and the next.

We begin with how we are sometimes controlled by our own beliefs and inhibitions or the power we have given others over us. Jared, age twenty-seven, realizes he is not really free. He feels compelled to stay in a job that has no future "but pays the rent." This fits with his lifelong "safety first" belief, a wise truth but one that can go too far when it crimps the full range of our freedom. Jared is also quite skilled in photography and has recently been able to sell some of his work. He is afraid to launch out on his own because of his fear-leading-to-compulsion to hold on to a sure thing. This feels safer than gambling on the success of his own creativity and ingenuity. Jared can take that chance and reduce his anxiety by using some helpful practices, such as those discussed above. He, and any of us, can make use of stress-reduction techniques that address our fear. We are then able to do the very opposite of what we fear, to jump without a net. We can launch out instead of staying put, letting the chips fall where they may. We can deal with the consequences of our actions and so learn to stabilize ourselves in the midst of any hazards that arise. As a result, we are dealing with our fear of not being capable of self-care—the origin of the compulsion. We now trust ourselves when we arrive at a threshold, when we find ourselves in a pinch, when we dare to take a chance. We keep noticing the contribution of self-trust to becoming free.

Jared is controlled by his beliefs. Some of us find ourselves easily controlled by other people. We may be in a relationship in which we are controlled by our partner. We may feel ourselves controlled by our children, our employer, our friends. These are all forms of compliance, the cancellation of freedom. When we allow ourselves to be controlled by others, we are giving up on our natural longing for liberty.

As we wonder *why* we let ourselves be controlled, we begin to see how we might be in on it. It seems as if we are being intimidated by those who are controlling us. We imagine that we are afraid of them. Yet, in reality we might be afraid of having freedom and personal power. In the poem by Emily Dickinson entitled "We never know how high we are," the poet delves into the question of why we don't stretch to the full dimensions of ourselves. She concludes that each of us carries around a "fear to be a King." In other words, we fear our own power.

Predators, especially in relationships, will notice that fear in us and take advantage of it. But as we look carefully at the transactions between us and them, we see that they are not simply controlling us; they are, on another level, *keeping us safe from the threat we feel about having a license to be who we really are.* By being under their control, we never have to face the responsibilities and challenges that come with free choice. Our fear is not about how they will harm or leave us if we don't obey them but about the risk of being fully free. *My fear is not of them but of me.*

On a related topic, we also notice that in civil life we follow laws that are just and reasonable because they are for the common good. However, there are unspoken laws regarding behavior and belief that are imposed on us within society, family, and religion that may not be for our best good. It is a task of healthy adulthood to examine these rules to see if they fit with our individual sense of personal liberty and happiness. For instance, we might have been born into a family that has inculcated rabid prejudices into us against certain groups because of their religion, nationality, race, gender, sexual orientation, or political affiliation. As adolescents and adults it is up to us to decide whether we will maintain those biases. This takes self-informing and deep examination of our own sense of what is right and good. It is only then that we are honoring our longing for true freedom.

The religion we were born into may have imposed such restrictions on how we think and see the world that now we are inhibited in imagination, thought, or behavior. It will be up to us to examine beliefs and moral proscriptions one by one to see which ones reflect our own values now. Freedom is moving from compliance with others to personal choice. That transition is what we long for. A healthy, mature adult will not be content to operate out of blind obedience.

Our gender-based behavior might also be highly regulated by societal directives. For instance, girls early on learn the carefully constructed rules about how a woman should look and act. This runs the gamut from having their hair done to needing to shave their legs and underarms. There are rules about which shoes to wear with which outfits, which jewelry, which handbag, and which makeup. The rules are exact, even extending to which nail polish goes with which lipstick. All these fashion and grooming styles, or rules, are rightly criticized by feminists as oppressive. Yet, we can also acknowledge that a woman might, consciously and out of personal preference, choose to follow some or all the conventions, and that does not mean that she has lost her freedom. On the other hand, women who choose not to follow the norms/rules represent an equally authentic model of what is included in being feminine.

The bigger issue for women is that the freedoms allowed to men—for example, freedom over their own bodies—are still denied to them in so many ways. Political, religious, and familial freedom for women the world over is still not secured or even widely acknowledged as legitimate. That calls for continual protest, and all of us can join in that struggle. All five longings are legitimate human rights, so all of us can work toward their becoming available equally to all people.

For boys and men, freedom to be themselves was perhaps inhibited by a set of imposed rules about the posturing that is defined as manliness. Such "manliness" is, of course, nothing more than a set of rules, directives, and restrictions we were schooled—or scared—into following. The strict code was inculcated by peers, family, society, movies. They fooled us into thinking that the macho-manly, often aggressive style was the right one for all boys. Unless we have seen through this imposition, we might still admire masculine-macho men and lament that we are not able to be like them. Their intimidating manner in any confrontation may lead us to believe they are stronger than we are, so we keep ourselves at a disadvantage in that way too.

The rules extend to every part of our lives: how we dress, how we walk or sit, which words or what tone of voice we use, how we gesture, how or which feeling we show, how we behave, how we are sexually. There are carefully drawn boundaries around each of these.

We had many models, especially the guys around us who gave the appearance of successfully living by the tribal rules. They formed an in-group and the rest of us were outsiders. Being on the margin often led to a sense of shame. We wished we were like "the guys," who appeared so effortlessly manly. Knowing we never could be like that pillaged our self-esteem. *But how free were the manly guys who had to follow such severe regulations?**

I have observed how the manliness rules-of-the-role in adult life can interfere with intimate relating. In my experience working as a therapist with couples on how to improve listening/communicating skills, I've sometimes encountered a man who will say the appropriate thing but in a crusty tone and with no eye contact. I can see that speaking tenderly is difficult for him. I am aware that one of his regulations is a John Wayne tone of voice. How much freedom does a man have if even the tone of his voice is carefully calculated by others? To be free is to have access to the full range of human emotions. We don't enjoy that range if our words, tone, and gestures are already assigned to us from outside, and ever so stereotyped, sources.

The character of Atticus Finch in *To Kill a Mockingbird* is a wonderful example of a manly guy who *is* tender in his speech and whose actions are not tied to the standard requirements of manliness. He shows us that manliness is not a combination of toughness and ego with a list of mannerisms and attitudes to be scrupulously

---

*I was introduced to the ideas in the above three paragraphs by my experience of the very commendable Breakthrough for Men program in Monterey, California, designed by Fred Jealous.

adhered to. It is unique in each man with an individually designed style of strength and sensitivity.

The psychologist Abraham Maslow noticed that self-actualized men and women were resistant to enculturation. Carl Rogers used the phrase "fit vanguard" to describe the self-actualized people who lead the evolution of our species into new freedoms. To fulfill our longing for freedom will take being ourselves no matter what the consequences, an enterprise requiring pluck and audacity. Here we see another example of how the fulfillment of a longing is in our own hands. We also see how the recommendations of the self-help movement regarding self-acceptance and self-affirmation are geared to the actualization of our longing for freedom.

From an individual-cosmic perspective, the exodus theme of longing for deliverance remains alive in us, as it was for the ancient Israelites and for the Civil War slaves. But in personal life, deliverance can only come from within ourselves. We recall Oliver Wendell Holmes, Sr., in his poem "The Chambered Nautilus" advising, "Build thee more stately mansions, O my soul . . . Till thou at length art free."

Finally, a bodhisattva is an enlightened person who chooses not to enter nirvana until all beings come along with him into liberation. In the style of a bodhisattva, our longing for freedom includes wanting all men and women to be free. None of us is really free until all of us are free. There is a direct connection between fulfilling this personal longing and dedicating ourselves to social justice and equality. We keep noticing that longings are not simply wishes for what we want. Each of the five longings is a calling to repair the world. This means aligning ourselves with the intention of evolution: more consciousness, more connection. Then our cosmic purpose is revealed to us: cocreating a world of love, meaning, freedom, happiness, and growth.

I have sworn upon the altar of God an eternal hostility against every form of tyranny over the mind of man.
—THOMAS JEFFERSON, Letter to Dr. Benjamin Rush, 1800

From Compulsion to Choice

Many of us ordinary neurotics suffer from compulsiveness in some form. A compulsion can take the form of a ritual that gives us a sense of being in full control. (How ironic, since they eventually control us.) Our inhibiting compulsions may have become so much a part of our personal landscape that we hardly notice them. For some of us they might be more than inhibitions. They might be subtle artifices to avoid freedom. Thus, by remaining tied to our compulsions we avoid the scary challenges that come with freedom and spontaneity. What follows are some examples of compulsion.

I have to:

- Keep feeding my addiction.
- Maintain my habits.
- Remain loyal to my routine.
- Get it done, get it over with, get to the end of whatever I am doing no matter how stressful that may become.
- Keep commitments "even if it kills me."
- Leave nothing unfinished once I have started it, even if finishing it holds up some other important task.
- Fastidiously keep everything neatly in its exact place.
- Check and recheck appliances before leaving the house.
- Be on time every time.
- Be serious at all times: I can't be frivolous in any way, no matter how briefly. Everything I do has to be purposeful. I can't just do nothing. Even if I go for a walk, it has to be for exercise or to get somewhere. I have to use my time well; no daydreaming, reveries, meandering, sitting around, gazing out the window.
- Save or hoard useless items (or I might instead find satisfaction in getting rid of things).
- Caretake others with the motive of governing them and of assuring myself they will be cared for according to my wishes or standards.

- Be a religious fundamentalist or hold on to beliefs inherited
  from my childhood religion rather than keep up with new
  theological ideas and appreciate the contributions of traditions
  other than my own.
- Be and stay in control at all times.

*With compulsions like these how much of my life is really mine?
What happens to my longing for freedom if I remain so bound and
obligated? Freedom can be nothing less than liberation from all
attachments that hold me hostage.*

In this section, I am not referring to the mental illness called
obsessive-compulsive disorder. This is an anxiety disorder in which
someone is at the mercy of unwanted thoughts and fears. The obsession pushes her to perform compulsive acts or rituals meant to
reduce the anxiety. An obsessed person might know that the compulsive action is unreasonable but still can't help but engage in it. In
fact, the anxiety increases when she fails to do so.

The treatment for this disorder is often medication that helps
reduce anxiety. Secondly, people benefit from cognitive behavioral
therapy, especially exposure and response prevention. "Exposure"
refers to contact with what we fear so that it can become safer to us.
"Response prevention" means no longer being forced to act in the
usual compulsive way. For instance, someone might be obsessed
with a fear of germs that might attack her from handling doorknobs
or other objects. She can learn gradually to expose herself to what
she fears is contaminated. Her use of stress-reduction techniques
helps her deal with the increased anxiety. Little by little, she notices
that there is no harm or damage to her after all. She then gradually
forgoes the habitual, anxiety-reducing ritual of using a handkerchief
on a doorknob and/or washing her hands immediately afterward.
The obsession and compulsion subside. The illness may not evapo-
rate fully, but it can be managed by commitment forms of therapy
like these.

We who do not suffer so severely can work with our more man-
ageable compulsions in three ways:

- We practice mindfulness and stress-reduction techniques.
- We identify the fear behind our compulsion and work with ways to reduce or end it.
- We forgo performing or completing our ritual behavior, acting as if we believe there were no real threat.

Here is an example: We feel compelled to finish a task once we start it even if something more important awaits us. We *have to* wash, dry, and put away *all* the dishes before we leave the house, even though we are already late for work. Using this three-part practice, we take a deep breath, noticing our inhalation and exhalation, and consciously choose not to complete the task for now. When we return home, we do the cleaning without rushing through it, perhaps with relaxing music in the background. We then notice that nothing terrible has happened to us or to the dishes. Each time we practice these three steps, we will have less anxiety.

There is a deeper benefit to the breath part of the practice. This applies to any awareness of breathing. To notice and stay with our inhalation and exhalation is a living metaphor. We are noticing and aligning with the natural ebbs and flows of any experience. We then engage better with anything that happens, since all happenings combine ebbs and flows. This is a path to equanimity, the ability to go with what happens rather than dam the flow.

The Compulsion to Be in Control

Being controlling is a compulsion that is difficult for our partners, our family, our friends, our work mates. We can't help but try to take charge, to tell people what to do and how to do it, to micromanage, to oversee others' behavior, to judge them for not being what we want them to be. We *have to* get things to come out our way. This is not pleasant for them or for us either.

Control of others is certainly a trust issue since we believe that no one can be trusted to do things as well as we can. Our compulsion to control thereby isolates us. We wind up doing many tasks ourselves because we don't trust others to do them as we know they should be done. In addition, we are controlled by our own controlling, because we are indeed *forced* to take control in any situation.

Control is also connected with fear:

- We feel afraid of what might happen, so we try to establish control to prevent it. *Fear leads to control.*
- We know something is coming up or happening over which we have no control, so we become afraid. *No control leads to fear.*

In either case the fear destabilizes us and we feel physically raw, jittery, and anxious, with a sense that everything is falling apart. This is happening because so much of our safety and security have been directly tied to being in control. Control has become so much a part of our identity that when it flags, we lose our sense of self.

This predicament is based on several ways in which we are avoiding reality:

- We are avoiding the given that we are not always in control, that things can happen that we won't like.
- We are avoiding an unconditional yes to things as they are.
- We are avoiding feeling the grief that comes with what we might lose or lose out on.
- We are avoiding the sense of shame that we are unable to handle things.
- We are avoiding letting the chips fall where they may.
- We are avoiding asking for support. We mistakenly think that everything depends on us. We forget that fear increases in isolation. We forget our linked existence, the resource that can do so much to assuage our fear.

Ironically, if these four avoidances turned into practices, we would be free of fear and the compulsion to control!

Reducing our controlling style is the equivalent of honoring our longing for freedom. Our worry that things will fall apart if we are not in charge can bow to a new option, a practice of three steps: Yes, Trust, Let:

Yes: We unconditionally accept the givens that not everything will go our way, not everyone will do things as we want them done—especially our children.

Trust: We build trust in others by relying on them more and more. We listen to them rather than tell them. We give up micromanaging.

Let: We let the chips fall where they may rather than arranging how they will fall. We then make the best of how they fell. We are respecting the way in which reality shapes itself and our own ability to deal with it. Now we are indeed developing self-trust, the very thing we lacked to begin with and which made us so controlling. We are no longer afraid of what might happen. That self-defeating fear was what made controlling seem necessary all along.

Here are affirmations that support our practice:

- I let go of having to be in control and thereby find the power to handle what comes my way.
- I am open to grieving my losses.
- I say yes to life as it is, events as they happen, and people as they are.
- I let the chips fall where they may and I trust myself to make the best of how they fall.

When we face the limitations of our power and control, all we can skillfully do is bow to that moment. The conceit of self is challenged and eroded not only by the circumstances of our lives but also by our willingness to meet those circumstances with grace rather than with fear.

—CHRISTINA FELDMAN, "Long Journey to a Bow"
Tricycle, Fall 2008

7

Our Longing for Happiness

For the caravan of beings traveling on the path of mundane existence . . . it is the feast of happiness that satisfies all who have come as guests.

—SHANTIDEVA, *The Way of the Bodhisattva*

We begin by reminding ourselves that all five of our basic longings hook up to one another. Our longing for happiness is thus closely tied to the other four central longings: We are happy when are loved. We are happy when our life has meaning, especially when we are of service to others. We are happy when we are free. We are happy when we notice ourselves progressing, feel ourselves evolving.

In Greek the word *hedonia* refers to enjoying pleasure. We find it through our senses, for example, the pleasure of tastiness in food we enjoy. Pleasure is immediate and has a beginning, middle, and end. *Eudaimonia* refers to something deeper, the satisfying joy of living a good life and thriving in well-being. It is an ongoing happiness underlying our experiences and moods. Pleasure is about sensation. Happiness is not limited to sensation, though it can include it. We desire pleasure; we long for happiness. For Aristotle in the *Nicomachean Ethics,* eudaimonia is not as much a state of being as an activity, or choices that lead to a sense of fulfillment. For him, happiness is a combination of well-being, the good life, and doing good. We are happy when we make rational, purpose-oriented choices and act virtuously.

Happiness is generally thought of as a state of pleasure or pleasurable satisfaction. Happiness is the result of our possession or attainment of what is good. Joy happens in us when we are *glad* that something good or satisfying is happening. Thus, happiness is a consequence and joy is a response. We long for happiness; we feel joy when it happens. As social beings, we are joyous when we feel connection. Since we are always connected to the vast web of life and beings, joy is always alive in us and awaiting our awareness of it. The Hindu concept of *lila,* "joyous and playful participation in the spiritual world," is a way of expressing how joy and fellowship play together happily.

From the neuronal point of view, we recall the distinction between oxytocin and dopamine experiences: In authentic bonding we feel the release of oxytocin, the hormone of connection. This happens when we feel trust, resonance, a sense of belonging, a warm and homey feeling, a secure sense of inner peace, a reliable flow of the five *A*'s between us. We feel contentment, which makes us want to stay in a relationship and commit ourselves to it. We see the connection between inner peace and ease in love in this passage from *A Guide to True Peace,* a book published in 1815 by Quakers William Backhouse and James Janson: "Tempests never reach into that serenest heaven within where pure and perfect love resides."

Dopamine is the hormone related to the anticipation of reward, excitement, pleasure, thrill. In dopamine moments we seek pleasure; in oxytocin hours we enjoy connectedness. Dopamine is related to what we *do,* and thus the very seeking of it can become an addiction itself. Oxytocin is about what we *are,* so it does not lead to an addictive response. Dopamine leads us to attach to the rewarding object but not stay with it. Wanting a dopamine rush makes us want to seek again, a new thrill in new arms. Oxytocin leads us to stay put and to be so focused on our partner that we no longer turn our heads to stare at others. This combination of staying and attentiveness increases the depth in our bond. We might say, in summary, that dopamine gets us going and oxytocin keeps us where we arrived. Craving is a search for dopamine; ache and loneliness are the longing for oxytocin. Dopamine makes us want and hunt for the next high; oxytocin makes us want nothing but to stay.

This hormonal difference reminds us that happiness and pleasure can include both lively excitement and serene composure. Both are appealing, though each needs to be situation appropriate. We don't want inner peace at a football game; we do want it at bedtime. We want to be scared at a horror movie; we don't want to be scared at the dinner table. When we long for the happiness of serenity, we are longing for safety and security, contentment, inner peace, balance, harmony, equanimity, equilibrium, ease, well-being, composure, a flowing with what happens, a capacity for satisfaction.

The happiness in a secure relationship is one characterized by the five *A*'s, the components of love and simultaneously our basic needs in relationships. Since happiness is about fulfilling our needs, we are happiest—feeling the secretion of oxytocin—when we are giving and receiving the five *A*'s. Our happiness shows itself equally when we give those same five *A*'s to ourselves. Attention, acceptance, appreciation, affection, allowing are thus also the components of happiness, felt in oxytocin-enriched moments. These are moments of happiness in bonding with others whom we trust will be there for us.

The five *A*'s also reflect the difference between pleasure and happiness. Pleasure is momentary and based on satisfaction gained from externals. Happiness is ongoing and interiorly secure. The five *A*'s bring moments of pleasure as well as continuing joy. They represent our wholeness since they combine *hedonia* and *eudaimonia*.

Since the five *A*'s are shown and felt in ways that are unique to us, they confirm us in our very being as unique individuals. We can explore how each *A* relates to our happiness. We will see this in three directions: from others to us, from us to others, from ourselves to ourselves:

Attention is an engaged focus. Those who love us are absorbed in who we are; we are absorbed in who they are; we are absorbed in who we are. All three of these directions of our focus bring joy. Our ego concerns drop away when we are concentrating in a caring way on someone else. When others concentrate on us in an interested and engaged way, we feel cared about. Our attention to ourselves is caring about who we are and what we are becoming. To pay attention to ourselves is therefore a form of love. In addition, when we focus on our own interior life, we enter a jubilant world beyond our limited ego. We are in the realm of our higher self, transcending the immediate in favor of the limitless. We have found cosmic consciousness, an ecstatic experience indeed.

Acceptance by others is hospitality given to us exactly as we are, nothing about us judged, nothing in us rejected. We are happy because we are unconditionally received into the heart of another. There is room for all that we are in that cradle of caring from heart to heart. We feel comfort and serene delight. When we can accept others as they are, we feel released from constriction because we have opened to them. Openness to others is a form of happiness because it gives us a sense of the bigness our hearts are capable of. Self-acceptance is an unconditional assent, a total yes, to who we are. We are on our own side, standing up for ourselves. We do not put ourselves down for the traits in us that seem unsightly. This is the joy of being comfortable in our own skin.

Appreciation is valuing and noticing all we have to offer. When others appreciate us, we are glad because they are recognizing the value of what we bring to the table. This gives us a sense of worth and we feel proud of ourselves. When we appreciate others, we notice how they take to it and how they show us more love in return, a source of exhilaration. Self-appreciation is cherishing and valuing ourselves. We look back at what we have done and how we have become more loving, more wise in so many ways, and we give ourselves credit for that growth. We respect ourselves for our interest in evolving, for the virtues we practice, and the changes we have made in ourselves. If all we have to be proud of is that we are still trying, we can appreciate our good intention. That feeling good about ourselves is personal happiness; it is what raises our self-esteem.

Affection is showing our caring connection in emotional as well as physical ways. As we saw above, when others act affectionately toward us, we feel an inflow of oxytocin, the hormone of connecting and relating. We give that same energy to others when we show them affection. Affection toward ourselves is caretaking our bodies by a commitment to a program of health. We do not harm our bodies with substances or activities that cause harm. In addition to our commitment to health habits we also pamper our bodies often with whatever makes us feel less stressed physically. We show affection to ourselves psychologically in three ways: We handle and resolve conflicts; we do not stay long in situations—such as jobs or relationships—that exhaust our inner resources; we feel self-compassion toward our own inadequacies. Caring about our own welfare in such ways is a conduit to bliss.

Allowing is honoring others' freedom rather than trying to control them. When people support our choices rather than stand in the way of them, we feel buoyed up. When people see the importance of our deepest needs, values, and wishes, we feel confirmed in having them. When we honor the choices of others, we realize we have the capacity to love. In addition, we are free of the burden of trying to make them do what we want or choose what we think best. That abdication of control is a source of happiness indeed, both to them and to us. We also honor our own freedom by taking the steps that launch us into the life and lifestyle we truly want. We are not under the thumb of any person or institution. We are making the choices that reflect who we are, not the choices meant to appease or obey the directives of others. This brings with it the joy of being ourselves.

Finally, as beings in connection with others we cannot be fully happy while others suffer. Once we see meaning in life and in all events, we don't feel satisfied only with inner peace; we want world peace. Our loving-kindness includes a sense of caring about the welfare of the planet and the happiness of all beings. This honors the deeply forged link between individuals and the human collective. In Buddhist teaching, wanting happiness for all is *how* we find it for ourselves.

> May their joy be undiminished;
> May they taste of unsurpassed beatitude

In constant and unbroken continuity.
And now as long as space endures,
As long as there are beings to be found,
May I continue likewise to remain here
To drive away the sorrows of the world.
—SHANTIDEVA, *The Way of the Bodhisattva*

Preventing Our Own Happiness

When it comes to each of the five longings, we ourselves sometimes get in the way of finding the happiness we yearn for. We might be afraid to take leave of painful circumstances. We might be discontented with what we have, with who we are, with how things are shaping up.

Gratitude about what we have and are implies that that is enough. Here is the happiness of an unconditional yes to life as it is. Unhappiness is based on a no to the givens of our life. We then believe we are entitled to more. Again we encounter the word *more.* This time it is not about the higher self seeking the transcendent. Instead, it is a reflection of our ego's insistence on having it all, all the time. The ego's belief in its own supremacy is thus itself an obstacle to happiness.

Ralph Waldo Emerson, in *Representative Men,* wrote, "Our life is March weather, savage and serene in one hour." Our life is not always June. We are born to have abiding joy within us, but ironically that happens only when we are gladly greeting all seasons. We are not geared to be happy, in the sense of glee, all day, every day. Such a state of mind would make us superficial. We might have thought we had the full range of hearing until we found out that dogs can hear more than we can. The whole experience of humanness means openness to and an embrace of the full range of experience and emotion. That can't happen when we are cheery all the time. We need some hard times in order to see more accurately into who we are and what our potential is, to be toughened up so that we won't break easily.

Here are some specific mistaken beliefs that become obstacles to happiness:

- It is selfish to want to be happy.
- We don't deserve happiness. Our purpose in life is not being happy but enduring pain.
- Pleasure for pleasure's sake is wrong or immoral.
- We have nothing be proud of in ourselves. We are low on the totem pole, less than and lower than others.
- We will never hit the high note or amount to anything.
- We will never find the man/woman of our dreams.
- We have a lot to be ashamed of, guilty about, rebuke ourselves for.
- We are not OK, and we live in a world where everyone else is OK.
- We are not lovable. Our life is meaningless. We are not really free, nor is it safe to be. We do not have the capacity to grow and evolve.

Regrets

Hanging out with regret is a common example of how we get in the way of our own happiness. The word *regret* comes from the Norse for "weep" and the old French for "grief." Regret refers to sorrow, self-recrimination that keeps coming back at us. Regret is thus a form of grief that does not move toward resolution. It keeps gnawing at us and seems beyond our power to control or end. We keep grieving for something we have done or left undone. Regret is actually a sense of loss, accompanied by disappointment in ourselves or dissatisfaction about a choice we once made.

Regret includes the feeling of remorse, sorrow, self-blame, or shame for an action or inaction. This differs from repentance, which includes contrition, atonement, making amends, resolving to act differently in the future. Such repentance is sorrow that is followed by new attitudes and actions that bring closure. We have learned from our errors. Remorse is sorrow without follow-up, so it remains unresolved. We feel defeated by our errors.

There are many kinds of regret, but two stand out:

Appropriate regret keeps us humble. It serves as a humbling reminder to us of a major misdeed or mistake, such as a wrongdoing that has hurt or betrayed someone in a serious way. In this instance, we keep feeling regret because full amends are not possible, so closure evades our grasp. This fittingly lasting regret maintains our awareness of our shadow side, hopefully so that we will watch out for it in the future. Our intractable regret remains, but becomes milder because we have learned from it and it has changed our way of acting toward others. In this instance, regret has led to an awakening. Thus, a veteran can regret what he did in wartime and later become a peace activist. His regret has led to a spiritual transformation and he grows in self-respect in the process. In this instance, *we no longer regret, but we don't forget what originally aroused feelings of regret in us.*

Self-shaming regret is beating ourselves up for minor misdeeds or mistakes, for example, financial losses based on personal error or a minor action that let someone down. This regret is an impotent grief because it is grief that prevents closure since we keep rebuking ourselves without surcease. Such self-shaming regret can take the place of apologizing and finding forgiveness when we have hurt someone's feelings. In the example of a mistake that led to a loss, such regret can take the place of appropriately mourning. Hanging out with self-defeating regrets interferes with the process of grieving and letting go. How ironic that regret is grief but a way of avoiding it too. We recall Shakespeare in *Timon of Athens,* "Men shut their doors against a setting sun."

Self-shaming regrets can also be pointers to the work we need to do on ourselves. When we are obsessed with what we have done, or have failed to do, we feel self-loathing. This futile regret reminds us to work on building our self-esteem.

No one has to live with regret. We can't change the past, but we can make up for it as best we can. Accepting that challenge is a path to the happiness we long for, because there is nothing left to rue.

> End in what All begins and ends in—Yes!
> —*The Rubaiyat of Omar Khayyam,* translation by Sir Richard Burton

Contentment, Courage, Wisdom

One way of experiencing happiness is by living by the familiar prayer of Reinhold Niebuhr: "God grant me the serenity to accept the things I cannot change, the courage to change the things I can, and the wisdom to know the difference." As with the other longings, happiness is a consequence, not a goal. We are happy when we accept what is, change what yields to change, and are wise enough to know the difference.

Acceptance is a yes to the unalterable facts about ourselves, our life, and our relationships. When we have fully surrendered to the conditions of our existence, we are no longer quarreling with life as it is but honoring its firm guidelines. We have given up the need for an exemption. We know that anything can happen to us. We have bowed in profound reverence to earthly conditions, knowing they can foster happiness, love, meaning, freedom, growth. All five longings hang on one unconditional yes to reality. In fact, our central yes to a life of wholeness is a yes to the five longings:

- In our longing for love we say yes to caring connection, to relatedness.
- In our longing for meaning we say yes to things making a difference.
- In our longing for freedom, we say yes to emancipation from all that has held us back.
- In our longing for happiness we say yes to the joy inside us waiting for release from inhibition.

- In our longing for growth we say yes to the impulse of
  evolution in us.

Courage to change what can be changed is the foundation of what
is called "the work." It is a commitment to three steps:

1. We are willing to look directly at reality and all it is saying to
   us. We are willing to see what is happening in ourselves and
   between ourselves and others. We are willing to stare our predicaments in the face and call them by name—a first step
   toward resolving them.
2. We let ourselves feel the feelings that arise as a result, no soft-
   pedaling, no escaping. We notice how our feelings might be
   reminiscent of those from our past. We notice how many story
   lines gather around the bare-bones reality and we let them go
   so we can be present to ourselves and our circumstances with
   nothing in the way.
3. We open ourselves to new possibilities; we are willing to make
   changes. We draw new guidelines, set new boundaries, make
   new agreements with those around us. All these practices
   foster resolving the conflicts that have been facing us. At this
   point, we feel the joy of completion, of having taken the bull
   by the horns and yet survived. We feel the joy of something
   new in our lives, a sense of having moved forward on a life
   journey of and to happiness.

The wisdom to know the difference between accepting and
accomplishing is also a form of joy. We feel the safety and security
that come with discernment of what moves us and what paralyzes
us. We know when to tug and when to let go, when to move ahead
and when to hang back, when to plunge in and when to stand
immovably on the wave-lashed shore. This is the joy of fully trusting
what Carl Rogers called "inner organismic wisdom." Wisdom is
nothing less than waking up from our doldrums of fear and craving.
We open to the sun that exposes all our illusions and self-deceptions.

We see at last just how our world looks when there are no screens in the way, just what we look like when the mirror is clear of self-deception.

The wisdom we find comes from the treasury of wisdom that has been gathered by all our ancestors and held in safekeeping for us for all these centuries. Wisdom is thus a grace, a gift we can't make happen but that happens in any moment. We are delighted to keep discovering this omnipresence of grace, a joy to the world.

8

Our Longing for Growth

A rose with all its sweetest leaves yet folded . . .
—LORD BYRON, *Don Juan*

Our longing for growth is about stretching ourselves, evolving in ways that actualize our potential, reaching toward what we imagine to be more, better, or bigger. These inclinations are natural drives in all of us. To respond to them takes a willingness to risk. We risk going beyond the comfort of who we are here and now so that we can explore new territory in ourselves and beyond ourselves. We might even seek what seems out of reach, what we thought was more than we could ever attain.

How ironic that on the spiritual path we are taught to stay in the here and now, but there is at the same time a longing in us to journey out. It must be that true presence in the here and now is not an either-or but a both-and. We stay present in the here and now and automatically notice ourselves moving beyond here to there, beyond now to next. Indeed, simply staying in the moment has its own momentum because every second escorts us to a new now.

There is something in us, an evolutionary urge, that *seeks* challenges and wants to grow through them. Quantum jumps in evolving happen on the heels of challenge. Something shifts in ourselves, or

113

someone comes along who prods or coaxes us and we move to a new edge. Here are some examples of challenges that can lead to growth:

- Issues that clamor to be resolved in ourselves or in our relationships.
- Ideals we feel drawn to live up to, including those inspired by people we admire and want to emulate.
- Opportunities that take us beyond our limitations, inhibitions, constraints.
- Projects that evoke creativity, ingenuity, initiative, innovation.
- Surprises that interrupt our routine and lead to new, surprising possibilities.
- Demands on us to bring out more talent than we ever guessed we had.
- Shocks that rattle, awaken, and propel us out of complacency.
- Beliefs and restrictions that had served to make us feel safe but immobilized us too.
- Our own resistance to take a next step, especially into the unknown.
- Being commandeered to step up to the plate or to put ourselves on the line.
- Seeing our illusions about ourselves or others dissolve.
- Having to deal with losses of what had mattered to us most.
- Finding that our world is not as safe or secure as we imagined and proceeding indomitably anyway.
- Realizing that our life now is too small to accommodate all that we are or want and launching out into what is altogether new, no matter how risky or intimidating.

We do not have to take on growth challenges all by ourselves. We can ask for help. Our problems can bring us closer connections with others when we ask for their support, use it, and show gratitude for it. Likewise, left to our own devices, we might not expand to our full potential and gifts. As we saw above, we often need people—welcome or unwelcome—to nudge us.

There are also people who may obstruct our path to growth. As we saw above, a life in which we are controlled by others, unable to launch ourselves into the world in an autonomous way, prevents growth. For instance, membership in a cult or in a relationship in which someone dominates us interferes with our personal unfolding. Fulfillment of any one of the five longings only works when it honors the other four. They all have to consent and align. This is why, in the examples such as a cult or a suppressive relationship, the longing for growth is subverted. Growth can only thrive in an orchard that boasts these four other fruit-bearing trees: being loved not as followers but as independent beings, having our freedom and unique sense of meaning and happiness respected.

The growing edge of human possibility is more than individual. It is the drive of evolution to move all of us toward more consciousness, more love, more bliss, hence toward collective growth. As we have noticed so far, all five longings are both personal and collective. All beings are with us in our longings. Our longing for growth includes wanting to contribute to the world's progress. This is a form of conscious evolution; we are joining the universe in its universal evolutionary drive. It is also an example of loving-kindness because we want our circle of concern to go beyond ourselves and our near and dear to include all humanity.

As with all longings, individual or collective, we notice the "beyond" element, the transcendent dimension that makes any longing a spiritual enterprise. The talents we have are meant to be the tools for such progress. In a 1966 interview, John Coltrane remarked, "I attempt to make music better than I found it." Coltrane is showing a concern for the evolution of his field, music. This is an example of an act of love, because his art is meant not only for himself but for the evolution of music and for us, the people he never met, all beings.

A Challenge from the Past

Our childhood needs, like all our longings, have a lifetime shelf life. Our first adult task in fulfilling what we can of our longing for

growth is to examine our unresolved childhood issues: We recall
what happened to us in childhood. We ask ourselves if and how our
parents fulfilled our basic needs, the five *A*'s: attention, acceptance,
appreciation, affection, allowing. We feel gratitude for how they did
so. We feel grief for how they failed to do so. We recall Shakespeare's words in *Hamlet*:

> The origin and commencement of . . . grief
> Sprung from neglected love.

We process our past with our parents by awareness of their love
for us and ours for them. Is that clear to us now or is it still mysterious? Here are examples of the beliefs we may have inside us:

- My mother/father loved me.
- My mother/father did not love me.
- I still don't really know if my mother/father loved me.

If we believe the first statement, we feel a sense of belonging, of
being held. If we believe the second one, we might feel like orphans.
If we believe the third, we might never know for sure. An example
of this can occur in a relationship in which we are sure we are cared
about but we don't know if we are *loved*. Likewise, we can wonder
about our own love for each of our parents. Is that clear in our mind
now or is it still a mystery?

Childhood abuse and/or neglect affects the five longings in us:
We might have been told that we were the cause of our own unhappiness, that we abused freedom by disrespecting authority, that we
would never amount to anything, that is, have a meaningless life,
that we are unloving and irreparably selfish. As a result, we might
now doubt that our longings are legitimate or can ever be fulfilled.
Now we see the importance of enlightened, empathic parenting to
our evolution.

As an aside, we can notice that empathy is not just a virtue we
cultivate. It is a long-standing bio-evolutionary capacity built into

the neuronal structure of our brains. This capacity has a survival purpose. Since we are social beings, we can only survive in a holding environment, one that provides safety and security. This takes mutual attunement to feelings and sufferings, which empathy makes possible. As everyone's needs are recognized and understood, the whole community can then share its resources to fulfill them. Such cooperation makes for surviving and thriving, and it all begins with basic empathy. *Basic* in this context refers to how it does not have to be perfect, only good enough. Soon, with spiritual practice, our empathy opens into wide-ranging compassion.

This is what compassionate communication from parent to child sounds like: "You are loved no matter what; your life has meaning in every moment; you are free to be your full self; you have a right to happiness and will keep finding it; you are always on a growth path." With this message coming to us, we thrive as humans worthy of the longings in us. We emerge from childhood into adulthood not with despair of ever finding a fulfillment of our five longings. We are still trying; nothing has forced us to give up.

For those of us who had an absent, abusive, controlling, or neglectful parent, physically or emotionally, there is now a dad- or mom-shaped hole inside us. In our adult relationships, we may use men or women partners to fill that parent-shaped hole. We know our yearnings in an adult relationship are about failed parenting because the needs are the ones parents provide, for example, approval, being seen, protected, nurtured, comforted, encouraged. Such needs are the first tip-off that our needs are parent shaped. A second tip-off is that when we find a taste of parent-fulfillment from an adult man or woman, we still feel desperate for more. So we know this is a dad-need or a mom-need, not a partner-need. Our original transactions with our parents did not end when we moved from their house. They are up and running in our adult relationships—both at home and at work.*

---

*In my book *When the Past Is Present* (Shambhala, 2008) I explore this topic in detail and provide practices that can help us heal.

The growth challenge for us is grieving the loss that the hole from childhood represents. We embrace our own grief by letting ourselves experience three feelings:

- We are sad about what we missed out on.
- We are angry at those who did not come through for us.
- We are afraid we will never get over it.

Everything we grant hospitality to becomes friendly. Little Sambo in the children's story stays to watch the tigers run around the tree and sees them gradually turn into butter. When we stay with, rather than run from, our tigers, they become what everything really is: something that softens and nurtures. We can apply this to the feelings in grief:

- I am sad and stay with it; gradually it opens into an allowing of vulnerability, a component of love.
- I am angry and I let myself feel it without going out of control or retaliating against anyone. I am maintaining a sense of power while staying connected too.
- I am afraid and allow that feeling; that is courage, a component of love.

Grief, no matter how freely expressed, is not like surgical suturing, which makes a wound disappear altogether and permanently. Rather, it is like embroidery, slow and tedious, and even after it seems done, we can still see the parent-shaped hole. But that is an adequate fix because it is all that can be expected in the brief hours of a lifetime. Our saga with our parents and their abuses and absences is too long to end once and for all. How ironic that finding closure with our parents is ultimately a longing, something impossible to be done with fully.

We are already growing as we nurture ourselves in a re-parenting way by the grieving of our past. Letting go of needing our parents, or their substitutes, to take care of us means standing strongly for ourselves in loco parentis. We use affirmations like these: "I give to myself the approval I need." "I give up seeking acceptance so desperately from this man, but I appreciate him when I get it." "I join this woman in giving nurturance to myself." We are then no longer *running after* someone we think will do it for us but cultivating a mutually satisfying relationship. We work on healing ourselves, and our partners support us in it. Our work, joined to their love, then reaches back to heal the aching emptiness from decades past. We are then free to be with others as we really are, with all our wounds. They are free to be as they really are rather than as stand-ins for our parents. All of us deserve credit for our limited but sincere skills in such tedious but rewarding embroidery.

As an aside, how ironic that the partners in our lives who were so flattered by how tightly we held them, how deeply we needed them, never realized that the love we gave them was not fully meant for them as themselves but mostly for the father or mother they represented in our minds. But, no rebuke, that was not fraudulent on our part, only a case of mistaken identity.

By a charming coincidence I recall Shakespeare adding his advice about expressing sorrow, anger, and fear—the three feelings in grief:

> Give sorrow words. The grief that does not speak
> Whispers the o'erfraught heart and bids it break.
>
> —*Macbeth*

> My tongue will tell the anger of my heart,
> Or else my heart, concealing it, will break.
>
> —*The Taming of the Shrew*

> Be that thou know'st thou art and then thou art as great
> as that thou fear'st.
>
> —*Twelfth Night*

Evolving into Adulthood with Self-Esteem

Adulthood is not synonymous with physical maturation. To be an adult is to be present in the world in a conscientious way, to establish effective relationships, to make responsible choices, to launch ourselves into a career or calling, to act freely and creatively, to contribute to the world around us. All of us have an inclination to health inside us, but some of us were so damaged in early life that now its call is well-nigh silent. Yet, the yearning can always be awakened. It does not sleep like a corpse in a cemetery; it sleeps like a bear in hibernation.

Our first developmental task in becoming adults is working on what still haunts us from childhood. We saw an overview of this in the last section. Now we explore what comes next. There are some basic tasks that face us if we are to become adult in how we live our life. Working on them is how we help ourselves fulfill our longing for psychological health and wholeness. Our longing is for the wholeness that is our birthright, but our legacy was often mismanaged by the people around us, from childhood on, so it is now up to us to manage it.

A primary challenge to our own psychological health is building *self-esteem,* a sense of personal worth. We can be willing to make the changes in our behavior and character that contribute to that esteem. We are finding ways to enjoy life without harming ourselves. We are respecting ourselves because we see that we act with integrity. We live by standards of honesty and loving-kindness no matter what others may do or how they treat us. Likewise, we like our accomplishments. We are taking initiative, staying on point in our tasks, following through to complete them. The pride we have in ourselves recalls the words of Henry David Thoreau in *Walden,* "Every man looks upon his wood pile with a sort of affection."

We build our self-esteem when we act assertively, not aggressively or passively. Assertiveness is stating our feelings and asking for what we want in a firm but respectful way. Aggressiveness is doing the same but in an overbearing or manipulative way. Passivity is the opposite: letting others walk all over us, letting ourselves be abused or taken advantage of, allowing others to treat us with disrespect.

We also grow in self-esteem as we take responsibility for our own feelings and behavior. We do not blame others for what we feel or for our strong reactions to them. We acknowledge the likelihood of three trigger points in ourselves:

- Our reaction might be based on seeing something in the other person that is actually tucked away in our own personality. We are seeing our own shadow side in another person, but we have never admitted to ourselves that we were like that. *Clue: we might find ourselves strongly blaming the other.*
- Our reaction might be based on our inflated ego, which feels indignation or competitiveness when others call us on our arrogant or entitled attitudes, best us, or show us up. *Clue: we might want to retaliate, the ego's favorite sport.*
- Our reaction might be based on a transference of a familiar scene or feeling from our childhood that is now being reenacted. The other person is treating us as one of our parents did and our feelings about that are still unresolved, so we overreact. *Clue: we might feel the powerlessness of childhood.*

As we grow in self-esteem, we are less vulnerable to the slings and arrows that come at us from others. They cannot get a rise out of us so easily. What people say becomes more like water off a duck's back than a tsunami that engulfs us. We take unkindness, discourtesy, barbs, in stride. We don't allow them to continue, but we can shrug them off. When people fail to acknowledge our feelings or our needs, we still speak up, but with minimal emotional charge. We are accepting the given that people are not always responsive with the five *A*'s—even in intimate relationships.

Finally, we build our self-esteem when we have and consistently follow a program for increasing our self-awareness. We then do what we can to resolve issues that arise in daily adult life, both within ourselves and in our interactions with others. Here is a summary of what that commitment might include. Notice that it is also what therapy is about, a support that healthy people take advantage of when needed:

We Look at the Truth about
ourselves,
what is going on in our lives,
what patterns keep recurring,
what may be keeping us stuck.

We Notice
our shadow side,
our ego reactions,
how what is happening now connects to our past.

We Feel
our feelings at a bodily level,
becoming able to express them nonviolently
without being destabilized by them,
especially sadness, anger, and fear.

We Change
something,
no matter how small,
so that we thereby grow in self-esteem,
build healthier relationships,
and have a happier life.

All this leads to the three tasks of a healthy ego:

To Form Relationships	*To Reach Reasonable Goals*	*To Face What Happens*
Why: our innate longing for connection	*Why:* our innate inclination to make a journey to a destination	*Why:* our innate realization that we are not immune to the givens of life

To Form Relationships	*To Reach Reasonable Goals*	*To Face What Happens*
How: we lovingly attach	*How:* we take initiative and then follow through	*How:* we accept what can't be changed and do what we can to change what can be changed
The resulting self-esteem is based on the fact that we are doing our part to have a bond that works and lasts	The resulting self-esteem is based on a sense of accomplishment and on how we are activating our gifts	The resulting self-esteem is based on trusting reality as a path to depth, character, and compassion
The path that then opens is to ongoing committed intimacy	The path that then opens is to success and continuing development of our skills	The path that then opens is to enlightened and courageous living
and we feel loved.	and we feel contented.	and we have equanimity.

Integrating Psychological and Spiritual Growth

> Each of us is aureoled by an extension of our being that is as vast as the universe. What we are aware of is only the nucleus which is ourselves . . . a whole which unfolds.
> —PIERRE TEILHARD DE CHARDIN, *Writings in Time of War*

We also long for spiritual growth. Spirituality, like longing, can be characterized by the word *more*. It is finding or going for more than what we usually content ourselves with. A spiritual practice is one that takes us a step beyond our usual way of behaving. We commit ourselves to more than we usually expected of ourselves in the psychological realm. For example, when we are on the spiritual path, ethics and compassion become important to us. The spiritual takes us a step beyond the psychological while combining the two dimensions. For instance, we want to grow in self-esteem. That includes a sense of pride in our accomplishments. Spirituality invites us to go the next step and orient our accomplishments toward helping others, not just ourselves. We thus combine psychological and spiritual growth by widening the purpose of self-esteem.

Henry Miller, in *The Colossus of Maroussi,* shared a mystical experience when visiting Greece: "At Epidauros, in the stillness, in the great peace that came over me, I heard the heart of the world beat. I know what the cure is: it is to give up, to relinquish, to surrender, so that our little hearts may beat in unison with the great heart of the world." This is cosmic consciousness. Our deepest longing for growth is about expanding our sense of who we are so that we feel that we are part of an ever-evolving universe. This means being a contributor to ongoing cosmogenesis, the way in which the universe is continually evolving, being renewed, reborn, reconstituted. When religious people use the phrase "born again," I wonder how many realize our rebirth is cosmic, not only individual.

Our longing for more means no longer seeing ourselves as measured by our height and weight. Cosmically, we extend into the farthest reaches of the starry universe, as mystics have assured us. Here is a quotation from a sermon by Origen, a third-century theologian: "You have within yourself the herds of cattle, flocks of sheep, and the fowls of the air. You are a world in miniature with a sun, a moon, and many stars."

Buddhism offers us a spiritual program that helps us stretch in other ways. For instance, we learn to let go of grasping and rejecting. That is a spiritual practice, since we are going a step beyond the usual style of holding on to what feels good and rejecting what does not feel good.

On the other hand, Buddhism will not be enough for the whole project of expressing our wholeness. That project has to include our psychological work. Let's take as an example the basic Buddhist teaching about impermanence. We acknowledge that fact and thereby let go of the folly of attaching. But Buddhism does not offer the next important step, grieving what impermanence consists of: endings and losses. For that piece, we need psychology, which shows us how to grieve, as we saw above. We keep noticing that spiritual practice is not enough without psychological work and vice versa.

Using another example, we turn to the familiar phrase "Love your enemies." Psychology does not get us to this big-heartedness. It goes as far as facilitating awareness of intimidation by one's enemies, not letting them abuse us, and standing up to them assertively—all important survival techniques, all ways of increasing self-esteem. But psychology can't take us to the "more" that the human heart is capable of: generous love, inclusive and unconditional caring no matter how people treat us. For that we need a spiritual motivation, the result of a spiritual awakening. Our longing for growth, in this example, is a longing for what takes us beyond our usual limitations in how and how much we love. We also see in this example how Buddhism can complement religion since it offers a spiritual practice, *metta,* a Pali word for "friendliness" or "loving-kindness," to foster our commitment to demonstrate this unconditional and universally extended love. See the appendix for more on this practice.

Now we understand that we enlist all the sinewy powers of psychology and spirituality to fulfill our longing for the more that is wholeness. We can trust an ineradicable urge in ourselves to express the wholeness always and already in us, as husband and wife remind us:

> There is in the psyche a process that seeks its own goal no matter what the external factors may be . . . the almost irresistible compulsion and urge to become what one is.
> —CARL JUNG, "Concerning Mandala Symbolism,"
> *The Archetypes and the Collective Unconcious*

> An inner wholeness keeps pressing its still unfulfilled claims upon us.
> —EMMA JUNG, *The Grail Legend*

Moving Out of Procrastination

As with all our longings, we can be ambivalent about growth. Our commitment to our work on ourselves can flag. We might even be caught in a failure to launch. Challenges, from the past or present, face us and we put off dealing with them. We forgo chances to expand. We stay stuck rather than move on to what awaits and calls us. We don't take the bull by the horns. We don't say yes to the next chance to evolve. We procrastinate.

Our present knowledge of how the brain works sheds new light on why we might fail to do what we really need to do. We recall the words of Saint Paul: "I see another law in my members, warring against the law of my mind, and holding me captive." (Romans 7:23). The "other law in my members" may be the brain's limbic system, which includes emotional reactions. "The law of my mind" may be the prefrontal cortex, which is focused on intelligent judgment. These parts of the brain evolved in different eons. They do not always interact harmoniously, as would be best for us. It is up to us to weave them together coherently.

The limbic system is the lively actor. The cortex is the director. When they war in our heads, we are frustrated. For instance, when we want to get something done but we put it off, or when we want to follow a diet but do not stick to it, or when we want to stay away from substances that harm us but do not do so. Reading the breakfast menu, we certainly know that oatmeal is the healthy choice; we might say it is the one the prefrontal cortex chooses. But it doesn't have a chance against the possibility of pancakes and maple syrup followed by coffee and a cruller, the desires and delights our limbic system endorses.

Likewise, we have noticed that we are often adrenaline junkies. Using the same example, the oatmeal looks bland; the pancakes look much more appealing, especially in color, smell, and texture. The voice in our heads that says, "Oatmeal," is monotone. The voice that says, "Pancakes," is sonorous. Our mouth waters for the pancakes because our body follows our dopamine-pleasure choices faster than it does our cerebral cautions and recommendations. What the limbic side of us says also figures into the excitement: "Just this once, you deserve this, you can do extra exercise later to offset the calories." This is the voice of trickster energy, which works hand-in-glove with limbic responses, what are called "temptations."

The more evolved, human side of our brain—the cortex—has a hard time becoming as influential in our l limbic system and brain stem, the mammalian and reptilian layers ot our brain. Our thinking mind maintains healthy desires, wants, needs, thoughts, plans—that which satisfies our longing for healthy growth. Our primitive mind falls for cravings and appetites that subvert them—that which gratifies our desire for pleasure.

Our usual explanation of these contradictions between thought and behavior has been that we lack discipline. It is true that discipline can help us, but it is not enough and rarely lasting, as most people who have tried a strict diet can attest to. Our best hope is to notice our signals early. For instance, we are most resistant to temptation in the supermarket, when we can choose to buy cauliflower instead of cookies. Once the cookies make it into our pantry, we are goners. Cauliflower is the choice of the wise mind in charge; cookies satisfy the craving of the emotions that are taking over. The work is not to eliminate any part of ourselves but rather to marshal and manage these parts so that they work together and create a balance of what is good for us and what is pleasurable to us. That balancing favors our longing; imbalance topples it.

There is a Zen saying: "The horse arrives before the donkey leaves." This means that we can be enlightened before we clean up our act. The horse of enlightenment can appear in our lives before the donkey of work-to-do-on-ourselves has even begun to activate himself. In any case, we trust the horse of free-gift enlightenment, yet we still push our donkey too. Then we move from *procrastination,* a word based on the Latin for "tomorrow," to *destination,* a word based on the Latin for "purpose."

> Repression is not the way to virtue. When people restrain themselves out of fear, their lives are by necessity diminished. Only through freely chosen discipline can life be enjoyed and still kept within the bounds of reason.
>
> —MIHALY CSIKSZENTMIHALYI, *Flow: The Psychology of Optimal Experience*

Our Pilgrim Soul

> But one man loved the pilgrim soul in you . . .
> —WILLIAM BUTLER YEATS, "When You Are Old"

The recent interest in the Camino de Santiago pilgrimage route illustrates a longing people have had for centuries. The Camino is a path to the shrine of Santiago de Compostela in northern Spain. Since medieval times, people have made the pilgrimage to the cathedral there. Buddhism and most religions also recommend pilgrimages as spiritual practices. For instance, in Islam every believer is called to make at least one pilgrimage to Mecca in his or her lifetime. What is the basis for religious endorsements of pilgrimages? It is precisely our universal human longing for growth, for becoming more than we were by going farther than we ever dared. The longing for growth is shown in this instance, by walking from where we are to where something transformative awaits us. The destination of any pilgrimage is a new horizon, the one we glimpse and are drawn to.

We begin with a distinction. As we have observed, desire is for what is known and attainable. A longing is for what is mysterious and not fully attainable. We desire to go on a pilgrimage. We long for the wonderful and as-yet-unknown inner adventures that await us on the path and upon our arrival at our destination. For instance, when we reach the shrine, we might realize that we are not looking at a saint above us but looking into a mirror of our own always-sacred soul. Our longing for self-realization, the combination of all five longings, is the treasure we have then found on the pilgrimage. This is something we could not have known before we left home. Our desire contained the longing like a pearl in an oyster or a diamond in a mine.

Throughout the ages people have wanted to take to the open road. The pilgrim path is a metaphor for the spiritual path. We notice it is like going on a retreat, the sitting version of a pilgrimage. The motivations for both inner and outer pilgrimages have the momentum of a journey:

- Something in us just wants to do it and we don't fully know why.
- We are tired of our life routine and want a whole new experience and hope to find new perspective.
- We are seeking the answer to a taxing question or conundrum. We are confused and want some clarity.
- We are trying to discern our true calling.
- We are wounded interiorly or have an illness and we seek a healing.
- We have a devotion to the saint represented in the shrine and are going there to pray.
- We have something to be enormously grateful for and the pilgrimage is a way of showing thanks.
- We are making atonement for something—a common medieval motivation.
- We want to activate all five of our longings in a spiritual setting: We will feel the loving companionship of fellow pilgrims. We will find meaning in the experience from the first step to the last. We will feel free and yet have a path to follow. It will be one we choose but one that ancestors have followed too. We will be happy doing this. We will grow from the experience.

Nature pricks them with such passion
That folk long to go on pilgrimages
To tread new shores . . . to seek shrines far away.
—GEOFFREY CHAUCER, General Prologue, *The Canterbury Tales*

Assisting Graces in the Dark

Growth is not only a matter of effort in the struggle phase of our life's heroic journey. Yes, we fight with all our might. Yet, we also might notice assistance from forces beyond human making. This transcendent assistance is the grace that adorns our human journey. Grace is a gift of progress by quantum leap, unexplainable and not owing to any work we might have done. Grace shows the hero that effort and battle successes are not all it takes to reach his goal.

Awareness of grace assures the hero that hubris, egotistical pride, won't take over. Grace is how a power higher than ego offers us help. The hero says yes and thanks to such a gift. This acknowledgment of grace is a giant step toward spiritual transformation.

One way this realization happens in hero-heroine stories is by a dark time, paralysis of powers, a sinking into immobility, a vertiginous drop into empty space. The hero finds himself temporarily disabled, not in a city anymore but in a desert. This refers to the monochromatic time-out from external struggle when the task is to pull back from fighting the dragon out there and face our own demons. In an energy-deprived state we are more likely to let go, which is the best attitude in such a moment.

Hermann Hesse, in his novel *Narcissus and Goldmund,* writes of this time: "He let himself be led into the night, into the woods, into the sightless, secret, wordless land of no-thought." Our own journey toward growth will certainly entail a similar comfortableness with darkness and uncertainty. We might even voluntarily enter it as Walt Whitman undertakes in his poem "When Lilacs Last in the Dooryard Bloom'd":

> I fled forth to the hiding receiving night that talks not,
> Down to the shores of the water, the path by the swamp
>   in the dimness,
> To the solemn shadowy cedars, and ghostly pines so still.

Notice all the words in only these three lines that signify vagueness, ambiguity, mystery: "hiding," "night," "talks not," "shores," "swamp," "dimness," "shadowy," "ghostly," "still." And the poet *wanted* to go there. That is the attitude of openness to initiation. We can make this journey too. Indeed, we go unescorted every night into the strangest of lands, our unconscious, where frightening perils lurk and gruesome shadows seem so ready to engulf us.

Moreover, to someone with a fear of closeness, the possibility of powerlessness can be as terrifying as a nightmare: "This means I will need someone; I will become vulnerable to betrayal." Our first instinct is to gain control, thereby making the need for others unnecessary. To let go of control means becoming receptive to being helped. That is a fearsome option when openness has come to mean that our wounds are opening, with no sutures in sight.

Yet, the dark place and the immobilization are nothing to fear, nor are they signs of failure. This is an incubation period to ready the hero for the next great challenge facing him. The wilderness is preparatory, initiatory. The manna of sustenance does not fall onto crowded streets but onto the wasteland. We see examples of desert initiations in the Bible when the Israelites survive forty years in the wilderness; Jesus spends forty strength-building days and nights there before beginning his public life; Saint Paul goes to the deserts of Arabia for three years upon his conversion. Dorothy is put to sleep in a poppy field in Oz. Robin Hood is powerless in prison awaiting execution. In this phase of inability to engage in derring-do, Robin has to rely on feminine forces, as we see symbolized in Maid Marion helping him escape.

One final note helps us understand the role of grace in our lives. We recall film heroes of different eras, both with skill to face their enemies: Robin Hood relies only on his sword. Luke Skywalker has a sword, but he also has something much more powerful: a spiritual Force, an assisting grace he can call upon. This is a metaphor for the difference between believing we have only ego going for us and having grace assisting us too. Both Luke and Robin have full access to grace; both are surrounded by it. The only difference is awareness of it.

> I am not equal to my longing.
> Somewhere there should be a place
> the exact shape of my emptiness—
> —JANE MEAD, "Concerning That Prayer I Cannot Make"

9

Questions That Don't Go Away

> Gotama's awakening involved a radical shift of perspective rather than the gaining of privileged knowledge into some higher truth. . . . The awakening itself is not a cognitive act. It is an existential readjustment, a seismic shift in the core of oneself and one's relation to others and the world. Rather than providing Gotama with a set of ready-made answers to life's big questions, it allowed him to respond to those questions from an entirely new perspective.
>
> —STEPHEN BATCHELOR, *Confession of a Buddhist Atheist*

There are many questions that have plagued humanity for centuries. Two that stand out are: Is there a God? and Why is there evil? *Each is a longing in disguise.* When we ask, "Is there a God?" what we really mean is, "Is there a reliable force to turn to?" Under the philosophical question is a longing for a caring love that will come through for us. When we ask, "Why is there evil?" we mean, "How can I trust humans? How can I find safety and security in the midst of so much aggression?" Our longing is for love and trust. We shall explore all this in detail in this chapter. We shall see how each question reveals all five of the long-standing longings in all of us.

The enduring questions about life and humanity are enigmas, puzzling and inexplicable. They are conundrums, confusing but intriguing. Each is also a riddle. A riddle is a question that rallies our ingenuity and creativity because its answer is somewhere included in the question. For instance, "Why are we here?" contains an implication that we are indeed here for a reason. We can respond by acknowledging that we are here and that that fact is all that matters. Then it is up to us to make the best of our life for ourselves and others. We have found our response to the question by entering it more deeply than ordinary thinking might succeed in reaching. That style of entry rather than answer-seeking is what is meant by "a radical shift of perspective," a "seismic shift in the core of oneself and one's relation to others and the world," as Stephen Batchelor says above.

The enduring questions of life are also koans. A koan is a mind-boggling question that defies logic. The hearer realizes he can't answer the question using his ordinary cognitive skills. He can only give up thinking and stand in wonder. He can only surrender to his existential condition of cognitive limitation in favor of awe. He comes to see that enlightenment is beyond what the mind can help us find. An example of a koan is "What is the sound of one hand clapping?" There is no logical answer to this question since the very definition of clapping includes the necessity of using two hands. Two hands clapping is thus about dualism. This is symbolic of the situation in which I, as subject, seek something, an object. I can give up seeking in that way. I can then realize instead that I am myself the seeking, the question, and the answer all at once. That might be the equivalent of one hand clapping. I have now at least made somewhat of an entry into the mystery of nonduality, the equivalent of enlightenment. It will, however, always ultimately be bigger than my mind can encompass fully, hence it remains a mystery.

Throughout the centuries, great philosophies and religions have wrestled with the two enduring mysteries of God and evil. We see how Buddhism, religion, and secular humanism offer diverse replies. Secular humanism is a philosophy of life that emphasizes the value of reason, science, and naturalism over religious dogma, belief in the supernatural, or what seems like superstition in how we form our conscience or make our life choices. Ethics and philanthropy are valued but do not require religious doctrines to define or support them.

> *Is there a God?*
> Buddhism: No.
> Religion: Yes.
> Secular humanism: No or maybe.
> *Why is there evil in the world?*
> Buddhism: Humans choose to act out the three poisons: greed, hate, ignorance.
> Religion: It is a penalty for sin, a choice to commit sin, or the work of a devil.
> Secular humanism: It comes with human freedom.

Why bother with questions that have no answer? some ask. There are indeed no answers to life's enduring questions, but there are responses. There are no solutions, but there are choices. We can choose to engage with life while holding the questions, even though we are unable to answer them. In that sense, we act as if life has meaning even when its most probing questions remain ultimately unanswered. As with a longing, our option is not a satisfactory ending but a holding.

It is also intriguing to note that when we ask unanswerable life-long questions, we are not really concerned with philosophy. We are usually expressing *personal* concerns. When we ask, "Is there an afterlife?" we probably are not speculating about the nature of life and death in general. We are not asking if George Washington will live on or if the guy next door will live on. We really mean, "Will *I* live on?" This subjectivity applies to all the riddles of life. They are phrased in an objective way, but they imply personal concerns.

The puzzling questions also dare us to move from the first-person singular to the first-person plural, from "me" to "we." This is appropriate since there is no unconnected "I" in any case; we exist in nature as linked to all beings. With a spiritual focus, one that acknowledges our connectedness, the questions become calls to action: "What can I do that will make a difference for others?" Now we are asking how a disturbing conundrum can ripen into a resolve. For instance, the sad problem "Why do children starve?" can lead to the resolution: "I am now working to prevent more child hunger." The "Why?" has become "Yes!" to a calling, a summons to us. We reply with a practice of compassion. In this way, an intellectual explanation is no longer needed. We are placing our bets on the spiritual practice of loving-kindness, which silences all the petulant whys.

The Heart's Shy Reply

> The utterances of the heart, unlike those of the discriminating intellect, always relate to the whole. . . . What the heart hears are the great things that span our whole lives, the experiences which we do nothing to arrange but which simply happen to us.
>
> —CARL JUNG, Foreword to *"The Tale of the Otter"*

Definition implies limitation. In that way, it contrasts with depth and mystery. There is no final or definitive answer to the ultimate questions, because they are not really questions. As we saw above, *they are mystery teachings about the givens of life.* This is not "mystery" as in a "whodunit." It is mystery in the ancient sense of entry onto a plane higher than that of ego by way of initiation into an ultimately impenetrable meaning. In this sense, mysteries are stubborn facts; they do not allow a pat or linear answer. They do not allow satisfaction on the mental level. There is no "That's all cleared up."

A mystery is an invitation into a reality that transcends the mind; a problem is a challenge to the mind for a solution. Thus, a mystery

ble in science or mathematics; only problems are. A mys-
ble only in philosophy or religion, the traditional reposi-
tories of mystery. Philosophy responds by speculation, with no final
answer; religion responds by belief, what seems final. Yet, both philosophy and religion admit that doubt is a necessary and inevitable
ingredient on the journey either to knowledge or to faith.

In the region of mystery, doubt is indeed an appropriate response
to the puzzling questions we are confronted with. Faith, in this light,
is confidence that doubt is a path to truth. Indeed, the opposite of
faith is not doubt but certainty. Faith is trusting doubt to open for
us in its own time—and that may be more than the time we have.
The child's alternative is to soothe our perplexity with a set of reliable beliefs to eradicate our doubt. When we do that, we miss the
mystery, "the many-splendored thing."

To enter a mystery makes it no clearer, but it does make it more
hospitable. The meaning of a mystery is always both revealed and
hidden, coming toward us and going away from us, here and not
here, near and far, visible and invisible, suddenly present and ever
elusive. To use a metaphor for a mystery is itself dangerous, as that
gives the impression that the mystery is or is like one thing. A mystery is always about all things, no-thing. We simply sit in the silence,
and it becomes a little clearer without being totally explained.

In this chapter, we come from the heart, not from religion or
philosophy, though we do refer to them often. The heart is able to
accept the fact of uncertainty and nonfinality, the style of longings.
With heart and imagination we walk into the mysterious riddles and
find avenues there into what our longings are really about. Each of
the enduring questions contains enduring longings.

Heart and mind seem like opposites. Holding opposites means
creating a bridge between them. Here is an example of the transition
from the thinking, dividing, defining mind to the heart that abides
comfortably in mystery. Our logical, intellectual mind might say, "I
once was lost but now am found." This usually leads to why and
how questions. We can, however, notice another dimension of
knowing in ourselves. We can be comfortable with paradox and say,

"I feel that I am somehow now both lost *and* found." This does not lead to agonizing questions, only to a heart-understanding "Yes!"

Our self-identity is always in motion, a continual exchange with the world around us. It is like every cell in our body: engaged in a constant flow and relay of giving and receiving. This is our body-mind, not a noun but a process. The more we explore our interior life, the more we find a sameness with other humans, not a separation from them. Our true nature is the same as everyone else's and the same as that of the universe. Our body-heart-soul-higher self is indeed one cosmic reality. We recall Carl Sagan's words: "We are star-stuff."

When we see with heart, we open a space inside and let questions enter. We let them live there unanswered for as long as they want, even a lifetime. This is what is meant, as we saw above, by *holding*. We come from a sense of presence *in* the question rather than with our examining mind above it. In this context, certainty is at best an exaggeration and at worst a delusion.

Here is the chart showing some of the differences between seeing with heart—that is, openness to what is—and seeing with a mind that is content only with certainties. The more comfortable we can be on the left side, where the heart is, the more at home we are with life's bewildering questions.

Openness Leads Us to:	*Certitude Leads Us to:*
Appreciate uniqueness	Pigeonhole and categorize
Be flexible about and open to ideas, especially unusual ones	Stay rigidly attached to our ideas, habits, or interpretations
Become explorers: the journey style	Keep believing that we have a firm grip on what life is about: the immobile style
Notice an array of choices	Be suspicious of novelty or innovation
Be receptive	Stay tightly tensed and closed

Openness Leads Us to:	*Certitude Leads Us to:*
Be willing to run risks	Stay away, out of fear, from anything but the tried-and-true
Come up with creative responses to whatever arises	Keep going back to the familiar precedent
Trust our intuition, our inner organismic wisdom, our enlightened nature	Trust authority or what society dubs politically correct
Awaken our imagination by thinking outside the box	Stunt our imagination by staying well inside the box
Enjoy more freedom because we see in an open-ended way	Stay tied to a final formulation, an incontrovertible solution or a perspective with no updating
Build our sense of power and adventure by trying new things	Cling to a false sense of safety and security by remaining in our comfort zone
Revision institutions again and again as times change	Maintain institutions that hang on to atavistic views
Configure long-standing values and resources to fit present needs	Attempt to force old solutions onto contemporary needs
Be willing to scuttle what no longer works no matter how valuable it was in the past	Cling for dear life to what worked before, even when it failed us then or fails us now
Meet and dialogue with a variety of people from diverse backgrounds	Limit our connections to those who are known to us or safe to be with
Orient ourselves toward the future	Stay stuck in the past
This is the beginner's mind, which is open to enlightenment.	*This is the expert's mind, which has difficulty opening to enlightenment.*

We may find no satisfactory cognitive explanation of life's conundrums. But with heart-sight we can enter a lived and felt response into the questions. How? Paradoxically, we understand more when we state the question in the first person:

Is there an afterlife? becomes

1. How would I live into a bigger life than this one?
2. How can I live that larger life today?
3. What is my next step?
4. Then I reply from *within* the question as I say, "I open to a bigger life than this one, look for ways to live it today, find my next step."

Each step leads to the next and deepens our experience of the question. Here are examples of responses to the question about the reality of our larger life in terms of the five longings: love, meaning, freedom, happiness, growth:

- We are made for love, so we seek it from others and feel we are at our best when we show it to others.
- We seek meaning in everything that happens to us and around us.
- We have bodyminds that seem designed to work to their full capacity only in an atmosphere of freedom, so we strongly want it.
- We look for ways to experience happiness and seek it in the world too.
- We are here to grow to our full capacity and we yearn for the challenges that help that happen.

Riddle 1: Is There a God?

The question sounds as if it were simply about the existence of God, yes or no. But the real question is about ancient human longings for *qualities of presence* that have perennially been associated with God. They match the five longings. Here is what voices of faith in such a presence might say with regard to each of the five longings:

- I want there to be someone who *loves* me, cares about me, watches over me, and to whom I can turn as a refuge and source of strength.
- I yearn for a *meaning* in my life and experience that goes beyond my ego and my story, both now and in a hereafter.
- I want to feel that my *freedom* is endorsed and guaranteed by a divine source, that I am "endowed by [my] Creator with certain unalienable rights," as the Declaration of Independence says.
- I seek spiritual *happiness,* the abiding sense of an indwelling divine presence supporting me by grace and giving me inner peace.
- I seek spiritual *challenges* that show me how to grow as a human who can love more, have access to true wisdom, and be a channel of healing to myself and those around me.

All these presume a capacity in us for the divine. The theological term *capax Dei,* a capacity for God, is from Saint Augustine, who wrote in *De Trinitate,* "The mind is the image of God in that it is capable of [knowing] Him and partaking in His life." Mystics go on to say that all longings lead to and are for God. Yet we might also say that the longings within us, as components of our higher self, are themselves "God within."

Our longing is often construed as oriented to a God "out there somewhere." Paradoxically, when the longing is fulfilled, we discover that God is not someone else somewhere else but a oneness here and everywhere. That *presence of wholeness* is felt to be in us and in all the universe, fully enlightened consciousness, fully awakened wisdom, fully unconditional love. An example of this is in the mystic's longing for God, divine wholeness, yet God, wholeness, is always also within her, so the longing-for coexists with the fulfillment-of.

In our essential being beyond ego we *are* love, meaning, freedom, happiness, evolution-in-person. As we have been seeing, our longings in daily life are echoes of a wholeness within. There is an alternating rhythm in us of what we are already and what we are still seeking. What we call "wholeness within"—our true nature, our higher self—is certainly not always evident, yet we do have the capacity to trust its presence. This not-always-evident presence can be compared to our pulse. It is always in us, but we become aware of it only when we hold our fingers to it. We can do this at any time, but most of us hardly ever do so. Nonetheless, it is always ready at hand.

Here is a recent experience of mine that presents another example of the metaphor: I have a single photograph of myself at around age one, which has been familiar to me throughout my life. Recently, I scanned this sepia-tone image to save it on my computer. I also chose to sharpen it in my preview program. I pressed the wrong tab and suddenly the photograph appeared in color! I realized the color had been there all these years, but it took a special action to release it. Likewise, our higher self is in us always but only appears in special moments. And yes, sadly, it can also remain hidden for a lifetime.

On any ordinary day we might feel frustrated that our five longings remain stubbornly unfulfilled. Yet, in moments we enter a mindful—or unitive—sense of ourselves and the world and *feel* our wholeness. We also know of it because all of us have, at some time (even if only once), had a glimpse of each longing in total fulfillment. That can be enough to trust our inner riches ever after. A taste has made the implicit explicit. We recall Blanche's statement in *A Streetcar Named Desire:* "I have been called a destitute woman! When I have all these treasures locked in my heart."

In the faith perspective, longing for the More is *how* God is embodied in us. We long for more, that is, for the transcendent and immanent God. All our longings are for what people have perennially referred to as divine: something, we know not what, that calls us wordlessly, we know not how, to make us more than we are now. That something is the essence of all being and, at the same time, our own inner essence. The higher self of the universe is contacting itself in us, all being to every being, no division or dualism. The Sufi mystic Al-Hallaj said it well: "I am He whom I love and He whom I love is I. We are two spirits in one body. To see me is to see Him. To see Him is to see us both." His mystic longing was for the companion of the heart, the beloved. This is the name of the higher self as love itself, what we mean by "God is love." This makes love itself a spiritual experience since any experience of love is an experience of the divine. Likewise, our longing for love is part of nature since both are about connection.

We might then go on to say that all our longings are spiritual, so we can therefore feel a reverence for them and for ourselves. We are the tabernacles in which immortal longings abide. Each of us is how God becomes personal.

God is not some big guy up there somewhere. God is a Yes to questions like these: Is there a source I came from and go back to? Is there a loving intent toward me in the universe? Do I have shepherding companionship so I never walk alone? When I am in a quandary is there a source of guidance? Romeo believed there literally was:

> May He, that hath the steerage of my course,
> Direct my sail!

Juliet asked if she could believe in a friendly universe:

> Is there no pity sitting in the clouds,
> That sees into the bottom of my grief?

Faith is trust that the five longings are the "right paths" to spiritual fulfillment. Many people have faith in a personal God, as we see outlined in the first half of Psalm 23:

"The Lord" affirms there is a God, a transcendent presence.
"Is my shepherd" means that this God cares for us and about us, that is, loves us.

"I lack nothing" means that we have all we need, no matter how deficient our circumstances.

"He makes me lie down in green pastures" means that God gives us the graces of safety and security.

"He leads me beside the refreshing waters" means that God reliably cares for our physical needs.

"He restores my soul" means that God reliably cares for our spiritual needs.

"He guides me along the right paths as befits His name" ("shepherd") means that God does indeed guide us.

"Yea, though I walk through the valley of the shadow of death, I fear no harm" means that a sense of the presence of God releases us from fear.

"For You are with me" is the high point of the psalm and summary of the entire Bible: God will indeed remain present at all times, abide with us through thick and thin, will not abandon us ever, though it may feel that way often. This trustworthy accompaniment is a central feature of the longing to be loved.

Thus, for the person of faith, the longings are for a transcendent source loving us, ending our neediness and craving, fulfilling our inherent needs and drives, giving us happiness and inner peace, caring for us, guiding us, freeing us from fear, remaining present, protecting us, accompanying us, comforting us. When we want there to be a God, this is what we want, just what we wanted from our parents. Fred Rogers, aka "Mr. Rogers," in *Many Ways to Say I Love You*, is referring to children but his words are applicable to all of us: "At many times throughout their lives, children will feel the world has turned topsy-turvy. It's not the ever-present smile that will help them feel secure. It's knowing . . . that they can count on the people they love to be with them until the world turns right side up again."

To ask, "Is there a God?" is to ask if there is a yes to our deepest longings. To say, "There is a God," is to reply with that same yes. Notice also that faith changes the very definition of longings because now they can indeed be fulfilled once and for all, either in this life or in one hereafter.

In mature religious consciousness we seek more than personal assurance. Our concern is for all beings, and our God aligns with the downtrodden. When we, too, align with them in our fight for justice, we come to trust in divine assistance. Martin Luther King, Jr., in his speech "The Church on the Frontier of Racial Tension," at the Southern Baptist Theological Seminary, expressed it well: "The believer in nonviolence has deep faith in the future. He knows that in his struggle for justice he has *cosmic companionship*."

Finally, in those with an agnostic attitude, we can distinguish two directions: God as nonexistent and God as absent. Some agnostics may wonder if there is a God. Others may doubt that God exists but also feel a sense of loss—as for a lost, absent, or desired lover. They might hope or wish there were a God who gives life meaning, a power higher than ego, a loving presence in the universe. They do not know if God exists, but are not indifferent about the value of "cosmic companionship."

Buddhist and Jungian Perspectives

So far in this section we have looked at the question about God from a faith perspective. How does Buddhism relate to the question?

In Buddhist teaching we take refuge in reality with all its securities and insecurities. The spiritual path is not about finding a transcendent being to trust for protection. It is rather a total yes to this puzzling and insecure world just as it is.

The legendary gods who appear in Buddhist tradition, such as the images of Buddhas and bodhisattvas, represent the energies of our essential nature. They are a hall of mirrors of our Buddha nature, endlessly extending through all events and all lives. Like everything, they are both psychological and cosmic. Since our inner life, in its deepest essence, is Buddha nature, inter-being, we are self-less, that is, never separate, always linked. Thus, our inner life is a center of all life.

The Buddhist teaching recalls the Jungian perspective of arche-types as elements of the unconscious life of all of us. Archetypes are dynamic forces, part of the very structure of our unconscious. For instance, the "good shepherd" image in the Judeo-Christian iconog-raphy represents an energy within the essential self of all peoples throughout the centuries. Since this energy is in all of us, it shows up as a common theme in stories the world over. It is usually depicted as a character, for instance, a helper, companion, rescuer, or protector. It does not have to be matched by a transcendent figure in the sky.

Shantideva in *The Way of the Bodhisattva* (Dedication 53), wrote, "May I behold my own protector with unobstructed sight." That protector will, in a religious view, be a transcendent figure—in heaven. In the Tibetan Buddhist view, it is a reflection of our inner protector energy. Thus, we call upon our deepest human possibili-ties when we "pray" in the Buddhist sense.

Likewise, Buddha and Christ, though they were both historical characters, can be configured now as archetypal energies in all of us. This is what we mean when we use the phrases "Buddha nature" or "Christ consciousness" as descriptive of our higher self. Then, in both religious and Buddhist traditions, each of our lives from birth to death is actually a lifetime of Buddha or Christ. We are here to let them incarnate themselves once again in us. In this perspective, to long for God is not to yearn for release from this life; it is to yearn to let Christ, Buddha, God live their lifetime anew in this lifetime of ours.

Yet, no matter how much faith we have or how dedicated we are to a Buddhist or Jungian perspective, we are often afraid. We might then still ask, "When I am afraid, is there a champion like the one promised in the Twenty-Third Psalm?" Ramakrishna used an anal-ogy that shows us two spiritual options in the face of such fear: When a baby monkey becomes anxious, he runs to his mother and clings to her. When a tiger cub is in danger, he can trust that his mother will come to him, pick him up by the scruff of his neck, and bring him to safety. Most of us are more like the little monkey than the tiger. We run to what we think will help us, something tangible, symbolized by the mother monkey. We might not trust that a power greater than ourselves is also present to help us, as in the example of the mother tiger, a symbol of divine assistance. In healthy development both orientations are necessary. We run to and are gathered by. We do what we can and sometimes feel ourselves access a power within that somehow gets us through the forest. We find ways to face our challenges and we trust we will be found and held as well.

The essence of us is not our story-self but our life in communion with all beings. We recall Buddha's words upon enlightenment: "When the morning star appeared, I *and the great earth with all its beings* simultaneously became Buddhas." Once again, we see that our individual existence is one with the cosmos. We exist in indivisible communion with the entire cosmos. Our true identity is not like fingerprints. It is like an indwelling. We inter-exist with all beings in a oneness of being. We are most ourselves when we live our lives in that style of communion. Buddha told us that was happening, and Jesus prayed for it too: "that they all may be one" (John 17:22).

> We are the *ones* we have been waiting for.
> —HOPI ELDERS

Real Presence

A belief in the existence of something requires only a cognitive assent. A felt awareness of presence happens as an experience. Here is a humorous story that serves as a metaphor for some diverse experiences of presence:

Miss Jones takes attendance in her high school senior English class. When she comes to Johnny's name, there is silence. She marks him absent on her list and states that aloud. Suzy raises her hand and says, "Johnny is not absent; he is present in my heart. I can feel his presence right now."

Some of Suzy's fellow students laugh scornfully; some envy her; some understand, because they have felt that same way about someone. These are the three main ways people often respond to our extraordinary intuitions: scorn, envy, and understanding.

Miss Jones insists Johnny is absent and tells Suzy she is wrong, that her feelings don't matter. The definition of *presence* for Miss Jones is superficial, materialist. It includes only physical presence, that which can be tested by the senses. Her view is dualistic: there is only one way for Johnny to be present, otherwise he is absent.

For Suzy presence has much deeper and broader dimensions. There are many ways for Johnny to be present to her. In fact, his physical absence is irrelevant, because she has transcended that limitation. His presence as a bodily experience in her heart makes Johnny really present to her. She, unlike Miss Jones, bases her sense of presence on lived experience, not on physical evidence. Suzy knows what Miss Jones means by "absent," but Miss Jones does not know what Suzy means by "present." Someday, Johnny may be gone or leave, and then Suzy will know about absence. Only when we have found the real one for us do we know what absence really means.

Finally, as a perhaps humorous aside, we can imagine a different scenario. Johnny is indeed in his seat, but his mind is a million miles away. When Miss Jones calls his name, he might honestly say, "Absent!"

In our example, Johnny can represent God; Suzy represents us when we have faith, trusting a presence even in absence. The reactions of others to the intuitions of a person of faith vary, like those of the teacher and classmates in our story.

In the traditional view of Providence, God consciously directs the historical process and causes certain events to come about. An alternative view is to trust that although anything can happen, there is a "cosmic companionship" that remains present to us in all events. It is the task of believers to find these events meaningful, to find challenges within them about how better to direct their lives in the face of them, that is, how to find God—or the Presence, higher power, divine spark—within themselves.

Finally, we can remind ourselves that in mature religious consciousness God always includes both the masculine and the feminine archetypes. Along these lines, the following story seems relevant: Buddhist priests in South Korea some years ago announced what was called "the miracle of the flowers" in the Jogyesa Temple in a suburb of Seoul. Flowers that appear rarely in Korea were blooming on the forehead of a five-hundred-year-old statue of Kuan Seum Bosal, the Asian equivalent of Tara, Mother of all Buddhas, also akin to Mary in the Christian tradition. Such blossoming is expected to happen when the next Buddha is about to arrive—in this case Maitreya, the Buddha of love. Pilgrims came by the thousands to see the white blossoms on the gold statue. Many are now comparing the site to Lourdes because of the healings that are happening there. There are twenty-one blossoms mysteriously growing on the five-hundred-year-old statue, which is regilded every three years and thus generally offers no place for plants to root. The monks say that seeing such flowers is like witnessing the birth of Buddha. The flowers are regarded as of divine origin and are known to bloom only when a great event for humankind is about to occur. This event is likewise an indicator of mature religious consciousness acknowledging the power of the divine feminine.

> The day is not far distant when humanity will realize that biologically it is faced with a choice between suicide and adoration. . . . Adoration is a surrender of ego so we can reverently enter inexhaustible immensities within us and things. It is our only fitting response to the depths in us and in nature.
>
> —PIERRE TEILHARD DE CHARDIN, *The Divine Milieu*

Riddle 2: Why Is There Evil?

Because the world is so full of death and horror, I try again and again to console my heart and pick the flowers

that grow in the midst of hell. I find bliss and for an hour
I forget the horror. But that does not mean that it goes
away.

—HERMANN HESSE, *Narcissus and Goldmund*

We want a world without a shadow side, one in which we can be safe and secure, one in which we get a fair deal. Behind the question about evil are our familiar five longings for love instead of hate, for a meaningful rather than a meaningless world, for freedom from oppression, for the happiness that comes from peace with justice. We also want to be people with the courage to stand up to evil and not engage in it ourselves. This reflects our longing for growth in nonviolent love.

We can't explain why there is evil. The option for evil choices is built into human freedom. All of us know we are capable of doing what is evil, yet we still remain puzzled by the question "Why is there evil?" Like all the bewildering questions about human violence, there is no satisfactory explanation. There is only a response in something we can do or be. When we encounter or hear of the horrible evils people perpetuate, we do not simply dub the perpetrators "monsters." Instead, we commit ourselves to a fivefold practice:

- We open to our grief about what they do or have done.
- We do all we can to right the wrong.
- We protest against violence and violation, but we aspire in loving-kindness for the enlightenment of both victims and perpetrators.
- As in hospice or hospital work, we stay with and nurture the victims who are suffering, without retaliating against those who caused their suffering. Our style is to accompany others in their dark valley, not punish those who blocked the sun. In this way we are choosing not the reptilian default path of revenge but the mammalian style of nurturance.
- We acknowledge the capacity for evil in ourselves. We can't trust ourselves fully. It will take assistance from a power

beyond ego to keep us on the path of gentle love. We ask for that grace.

Along these lines, we can recall that all animals engage in aggression but have no inclination to keep at it once they have established domination. However, humans have the capacity to keep hurting one another with no end in sight. We realize, then, how crucial it is to our mutual survival to acknowledge the shadow side in all of us rather than project it only onto the "empire of evil" out there.

Yes, there is a capacity for love in us. Yet, there is a capacity for hatred too. Both potentials, positive and negative, are opposites, and this is the nature of the human psyche. It is up to us to choose which part of us will emerge. Our work is not to kill the inner demon shadow but to befriend it so it can turn into an ally. Then we find its enormous creative tension and devote its energy to what is good for all of us.

Regarding evildoers, our task is to call evil by name and take a stand against it. We do this only to stop it, mend it, and invite the perpetrators of evil back into the human fold. In all this, we feel compassion for the fear and ignorance in those who are in the grasp of evil, because we ourselves have experienced moments of fear and ignorance and have been aggressive in our reactions too.

Good and evil can appear to be absolutes. Taking that view, someone is either all good or all evil rather than a human being, who alternates between acting from good and evil intent. In the good-evil absolute dualism it is certain that we will be proud to be the good ones while "those other people" are the evil ones. We are usually unaware of our penchant for projection, whereby we see in others what we refuse to acknowledge in ourselves too. This gives us permission to be adversarial. We feel justified in being violent toward those who have hurt us. As an alternative to "evil," we can use words such as *ignorant, unwholesome, confused*—expressions that lead to compassion and reconciliation, not judgment, recrimination, and reprisals. When we do this, we are upgrading ourselves as humans, rising from old ego habit to spiritual innovation. At the same time, we remain aware that some people, with full knowledge, choose to perform an evil action anyway. This, too, can be a call to compassion from us—while also being an alert to safeguard ourselves.

Some people wonder why there is no interventionist God who will step in and prevent evil or save innocent victims from its effects. From a mature faith perspective, we might say that when we intervene, God is indeed intervening but through us. We humans have three innate capacities: seeing, feeling, and acting. We can see, that is, we can recognize injustice. We can feel moved to take action. We can take action. (These happen to be the same three elements in an intervention with a family member on drugs.) From a spiritual perspective, these three capacities evolved in us to offset the givens of injustice and victimization in our world. We were made to work for justice and to help victims who are unable to help themselves. This is the equivalent, in religious terms, of divine intervention.

Our hope as and for humans is based on the fact that any of us can keep practicing the loving-kindness that is in us no matter what others do. Love can become stronger in us than evil or than revenge against it. Our faith in humanity is based on the belief that evil does not have the final word in the human story, that love will be tougher in the end than hate can ever be. We then choose repair rather than revenge.

What about our reactions to harsh or evil events that befall us? Such crises seem like reasons for despair, but they can forecast major changes for the better, become drivers of evolutionary change, ignitions of transformation. They can be the necessary factors in how major shifts occur. When all seems lost, or even when it is lost, we can trust that innovations shall appear, since necessity is the mother of invention. New visions impel our imagination and set the stage for a radical alternative—for example, the activation of a hitherto unknown positive potential. The bird that seemed doomed to perish might prove to be a phoenix after all.

A personal or relationship breakdown, or any overwhelming anguish in our lives, can be the threshold to rebirth. In a time of chaos a "strange attractor" can appear, something that elicits and facilitates a new level of order from the encircling chaos. This comes as a grace; it is not within our ability to plan or predict. We hear Viktor Frankl, in *Man's Search for Meaning,* describing an experience of this grace in a Nazi concentration camp: "In a last violent protest against the hopelessness of imminent death, I sensed my spirit piercing through the enveloping gloom. I felt it transcend that hopeless, meaningless world, and from somewhere I heard a victorious 'Yes' in answer to my question of the existence of an ultimate purpose."

Regarding our being victims of tragedy, "Why did this happen to me?" can change to "How is this *for* me?" When our suffering teaches us, we find an opportunity to fulfill our longing for growth. When our suffering leads us to care about others, we become healers, however wounded, a worthy albeit painful calling.

Finally, we can never forget that the human heart is like the Civil War general William Tecumseh Sherman, at times cruel, at times compassionate. The one who marched so unmercifully through Georgia was yet always touched with compassion when, long after the war, a desperate and bedraggled veteran of his regiment would show up at his door. The old-timer came because he wanted to look at Sherman once more and because he knew the general would never refuse a coin of assistance to a companion of the dark long-ago.

> We should not postpone and refer and wish, but do broad justice where we are, by whomsoever we deal with, accepting our actual companions and circumstances, however humble or odious, as the mystic officials to whom the universe has delegated its whole pleasure for us.
> —RALPH WALDO EMERSON, "Experience," *Essays: Second Series*

Loving the Unlovable and Forgiving the Unforgivable

> One sees one's heart in all beings and all beings in one's heart. The love is the same for enemies or friends.
> —*Bhagavad Gita,* chapter 12

Love your enemies, do good to those who hate you, bless
those who curse you, pray for those who mistreat you.
—Luke 6:27–28

On this linked-in planet, our relationships extend to all people.
Some of them act in unloving ways. We find it almost impossible to
feel compassion for them, let alone forgive them. In these circumstances we are facing a common spiritual challenge that arises in
relationships.

Our first question is "Is anyone truly unlovable or any action truly
unforgivable?" If everyone is a "child of God," or has Buddha
nature, then everyone is lovable, though not obviously so in every
moment. Then our spiritual practice is never to give up on others.
We trust the reality of an inner light in all beings. We trust, too, the
possibility of change, transformation, conversion, even when there
is little to go on in someone's present unappealing behavior. In both
instances, with spiritual consciousness, we trust Buddha nature in
all beings over the picture and history of the person we see before
us. We can also remind ourselves here that the term *Buddha nature*
is only figurative. It remains a mystery since our minds are not capable of grasping the full extent and depth of its meaning. Nor can our
vocabulary accommodate it, especially since there is no "it."

Some people who seem unlovable may have buried their lovability
in rage, hate, or violence, all based on fear and ignorance. They
evoke our compassion. Seriously criminal types certainly seem to
suffer from mental illness or brain dysfunction rather than being
simply evil. In fact, it is hard to imagine someone being totally evil
and not somehow mentally disturbed as well. This does not cancel
out criminal responsibility, but it does lead us to take the *context* of
criminal behavior into consideration.

We might say we "hate Hitler because he was evil." Yet, what do
we really mean? A person consists of the entire lifetime of himself.
Do we then hate the Hitler of age three or eleven? Or would we say
we hate him only from the age he began being cruel? If that is the
case, we don't really hate Hitler but rather what he became. He did

not act alone. He was given a mandate by many people to act out their darkest desires—some participating, some standing by silently. Do we hate all of them too?

Some people are consumed by hate and turn on others because of it. One reason people hate is their resentment that they themselves were not loved. Christ's command "Love your enemies" implies that love of those who hate softens them by taking away that specific reason to hate. People hate for other reasons, too, but this is an aspect we have perhaps not paid enough attention to. It is also true that some people only hate more when they are loved in adult life, because it reminds them of the love they missed in childhood.

We can also wonder if it is accurate to say that violent religious fanatics "have chosen the dark side." They were taught early on to subscribe to an interpretation of religion that legitimates violence. Now they sincerely believe that they are following God's will, doing the right thing. They are not like Hitler, who matured into evil ways over the years and then was given the power to act them out. This makes our question even more complicated.

We think of some actions as unforgivable. An act can be so cruel that it seems unforgivable when it first occurs. But it may seem less so when we examine the motivations, mental state, and background of the offender. In addition, we do not use the word *unforgivable* when we see contrition in an offender or when he makes amends. Something in us then automatically softens toward the wrongdoer. Shakespeare noticed this as we hear in Prospero's words in *The Tempest:*

> . . . they being penitent,
> The sole drift of my purpose doth extend
> Not a frown further.

A commitment to loving-kindness means taking the path of forgiveness. This means letting go of ill will, resentment, and the need for revenge—the components of hate. "Forgivable" does not mean excusable. We can forgive while still asking for accountability. Bishop Desmond Tutu in South Africa did not believe in the "unforgivable," so he worked with others on a plan to reconcile victims and perpetrators. This meant forgiveness from the victims and accountability in the perpetrators. The positive results show us that no human action is finally and fully unforgivable. (We keep noticing that the phrase "finally and fully" does not apply very much to human experience.)

Finding the capacity to forgive is a spiritual venture; we have to ask for help from a power higher than our ego. What makes us able to love the seemingly unlovable people and forgive what seems unforgivable is a grace that opens us to resist the vindictive ego style in ourselves. The ego does not give itself up; it takes a force beyond itself to get that to happen.

We find compassion for the violent, hate-driven ego when we notice the motivations behind human harshness. As mentioned above, they might be what in Buddhism are called the three poisons: greed, hate, and ignorance. To these we add fear. Recognizing the power of these four to move people toward evil choices helps us realize that any human being, including ourselves, can choose what is evil. This realization may help us access our capacity for compassion. The process will not be immediate or easy. We have to grow into that realization.

Finally, it will be hard to forgive others for their misdeeds when we haven't failed enough ourselves. The more our own shadow reveals itself, the more understanding and compassionate we become toward the shadow of others. It helps to ask ourselves, "When was I unlovable and unforgivable? Can I be, or have I been, reprieved? Do I believe that I can never deserve to be forgiven?"*

> What would people look like
> if we could see them as they are,
> soaked in honey, stung and swollen,
> reckless, pinned against time?
> —ELLEN BASS, "If You Knew"

---

*See the appendix for a practice of forgiveness.

When We Have Power

Any of us is liable to fall prey to the danger noted in the familiar and accurate admonition of Lord John Acton. He wrote in an 1887 letter to Bishop Mandell Creighton:

> Power tends to corrupt and absolute power corrupts absolutely. Great men are almost always bad men, even when they exercise influence and not authority; still more when you superadd the tendency or the certainty of corruption by authority. There is no worse heresy than that the office sanctifies the holder of it. That is the point at which . . . the end learns to justify the means.

Lord Acton's statement reminds us of the wisdom of our founding fathers, who so distrusted those with the power to govern that they set up a system of checks and balances. All branches of government are to be watched, audited, and continually scrutinized by one another. This is because no seat of power is immune from corruption. Corruption refers to taking advantage of one's power position for one's own gain. This tendency can apply to positions of power in political, societal, familial, religious, technical, and financial areas. Monetary gain is a key incentive in the pattern of abusing power.

People might engage in corruption by using their position to engage in graft, bribery, nepotism, cronyism, fraud, glad-handing, sweetheart deals, black marketeering, cutting corners, having one's "hand in the till," "greasing one's palm." Employees or project managers might bully, embezzle, pilfer, skim off the top, keep products that "fell off the back of the truck," cheat on expenses, spend company funds for privileged uses, act in cutthroat ways to further their own ambitions. Anyone in authority who takes a cut or looks the other way while others do it is also engaging in corruption.

The corrupting consequence of power is not limited to those who have control and authority. Members of an in-group, an exclusive coterie, a club, or an elite group may feel privileged, self-important, superior. This can happen in a family, at work, among peers, in politics, or in religious or societal settings. An in-group may look down on non-members or "inferiors" and believe they have the right to abuse, exploit, disparage, or lord it over them. Those attitudes are certainly examples of how power corrupts because they cancel respect for human equality and a sense of fair play.

Power is complex, especially since it brings us immediately into the realm of relating to other people. Whether intimate or not, human relationships automatically trigger subtle and not so subtle dynamics of competition, contention, aggression, envy, feuding, dominance-submission. Likewise, in a work space, for instance, our power as managers can be in competition with that of people who have issues with authority. The contest of power may have its roots in childhood or other experiences, and a resolution will then be even harder to come by.

There is no doubt that the inclination to corruption is a long-standing feature of the human shadow. So what is it about power that brings out the worst in us? The answer is simple: Since we are social beings, *we are not built for dominance power but only for partnership power.* We are not constitutionally able to be in full unsupervised control without harming ourselves and others. All control, power, and authority work best when they are shared and continually audited at all levels. Such checks and balances are necessary since all humans have a shadow side, an inclination to overstep boundaries.

On the collective level, nations can endanger world stability when they have unlimited power. As long as one nation dominates rather than partners with all the others, we are all unsafe. It follows, in addition, that true leadership ability has to be collegial rather than top-down. Our being born with leadership skills will not be enough to guarantee integrity; we can descend to corruption even more easily than others, because people keep smoothing our path to authority. They then keep trusting us rather than continually checking into our behavior.

Our leadership skills have to be heavily invested in an enduring commitment to egalitarianism if we are to avoid being corrupted by power. Domination is a shortcut to power; partnership is the long way home, that is, to the place of safety and security for all involved. In the adult world, we do not need leaders in charge except as guides and collaborators. We might then choose a leader/guide/collaborator who serves rather than reigns and who welcomes auditing of and transparency in all his dealings and ways of leading.

A metaphor that offers an alternative to the domination style of top-down is that of teacher and apprentice. The teacher shares what he knows and gives guidance, not to dominate but to upgrade the skills of his apprentice. Likewise the master is still learning new ways of perfecting his own craft so they relate as cocreators. The master-artist knows and loves the fact that his apprentice is meant someday to be a master too. This is the style of evolution toward equality, as in the example of a healthy family, not toward maintaining power differences, as in a fiefdom.

What can we do to be sure we do not fall prey to the corrupting influence of power? There is no way to rely on our own integrity alone. No one else has been able to rely on his or hers, so why would we?

One solution, admittedly top-heavy, for someone with political or corporate power who wants to stay on the straight and narrow is to hire a team of auditors. They become overseers of every decision no matter how minor. The team is made up of inflexibly honest people, not yes-men. They work on a voluntary, unsalaried basis. The auditors are people who cannot be bribed, will not "look the other way," "sweep it under the rug," "let it go this time." They do not wink at small infractions. They do not even fully trust themselves; they, too, ask for an occasional audit from neutral sources.

Yet, even with all these carefully organized controls, corruption is still likely, because no power on earth can override or cancel out the subtle and inveterate skills humans have in finding their way to the dark side. Our moral sense is too easily marred or numbed when we hold the reins of power. Shakespeare reminds us of this in *Julius Caesar*:

> The abuse of greatness is, when it disjoins
> Remorse from power.

From time immemorial, people who have abused power have gotten away with it. They are so often reelected, confirmed in tyranny
by the populace. This may happen because people in power rule by
fear not by kindliness. They intimidate us by creating enemies,
forces of "evil," that they promise to defend us from. This then gives
them carte blanche to abridge our rights in order "to look for the
terrorists among us." Absolute power corrupts, and unwitting people pledge themselves to those who have it. This is how fear and the
shadow work hand in hand.

At the same time, from time immemorial, criminal and immoral
people have seen the evil of their ways and atoned for what they
have done. Religion, rightly, uses rituals of confession, repentance,
and forgiveness to enact this archetype in us. Such atonement does
not, however, require a religious foundation. It is an inherent inclination, an innate need, in all of us. We can make a commitment
to atone: admitting our wrongdoing, showing sorrow for it, asking
forgiveness, making restitution or amends, promising not to repeat
our offenses. Twelve-Step programs have shown us the value of taking an inventory of how we have hurt ourselves and others and how
we can commit ourselves to making amends. A dedication to that
style is the foundation of any hope we might have in a humanity
with power.

Our spiritual practice can include acknowledging our own lifelong inclination toward dishonesty and remaining attentive to where
it may be lurking. We never have to act on our negative inclinations,
but we do have to watch out for our corruptibility whenever we have
power of any kind. We can refuse to fool ourselves with statements
like "That can't happen to me." It is a spiritual practice to accept
the given that power corrupts anyone and that we are not exempt.
We say yes to that and admit our need for help, both human and
transcendent.

Finally, we can look at one more intriguing fact about Lord
Acton, whom we met at the beginning of this section. He was an
observer at the First Vatican Council, which made a dogma of papal
infallibility. He opposed that doctrine all his life, though he
remained a Catholic throughout. Lord Acton is thus a model of a

person who can acknowledge and protest the fact that power can be abused in an institution while nonetheless remaining loyal to the institution. Once we get it, as he did, that no one escapes vulnerability to the corrupting influence of power, our heart opens—though our eyes remain open too—especially on ourselves.

Not that I have the power to clutch [hold back] my hand,
When his fair angels [offers of wealth] would salute my palm.
—SHAKESPEARE, *King John*

Epilogue: The Last Mystery

Lord, consider that we do not know ourselves, that we know not what we want, that we go infinitely far astray from what we most deeply long for.

—Saint Teresa of Ávila, *The Interior Castle*

Our longings show us what it means to be fully human. Yet, we sometimes don't even know what our longings are until they are fulfilled. From then on we can never mistake them, these longings unnoticed until met. Here is a story that serves as an analogy to this touching fact about us:

You visit your cousin on his vast sheep ranch in Scotland and while you are there, one of his border collies gives birth to a healthy litter. When it comes time to return home, your cousin gives you a wonderful gift, one of the pups. You name him Shepherd and are very happy to have him. You bring your puppy to your apartment in Manhattan. You certainly love him; you put him on a scientifically sound diet; you bring him to an accomplished veterinarian for regular checkups; you hire an experienced dog walker for him while you are at work; you yourself walk with him in Central Park every weekend. Shepherd has all a New York dog could ever want, but there is

161

something inside him that remains unsatisfied. There is a sheep-shaped hole in Shepherd—how ironic his name. He can be happy, but he can never be content, nor can he guess why.

A couple of years later, you go back to your cousin's ranch, bringing Shepherd with you. The minute those four little paws hit the ground, Shepherd picks up on a scent he was born to know. He sees his brothers and sisters herding the sheep and rushes without hesitation to join them. He feels true excitement for the first time in his life. Now at last he knows what was missing all this time; he has found what he was born to be; he is doing what he was given a lifetime to do; he knows the meaning of his name. And he will never want to go back to his old life, so luxurious, so ultimately empty.

Unlike Shepherd we have not just one but at least five holes in us: love-shaped, meaning-shaped, freedom-shaped, happiness-shaped, and growth-shaped. For each of these we have a profound longing, whether or not we can always call it by name. We were born to be something uniquely individual, uniquely human—all spelled out by our five longings. We will always feel something is missing if we have not yet found its fulfillment or if we have swerved away from it once found. We feel at our best when we find the lifestyle, relationship, and career that accommodates all five of our basic longings—at least in a good-enough way.

For little Shepherd it was easy to find perfect fulfillment. He has only to stay in Scotland and he will find fulfillment for a lifetime. We humans, on the other hand, can only feel our fulfillment for a moment here or there, hit or miss, not always here, not always there, anywhere but nowhere too. We feel a longing for many years; we find fulfillment for an hour. Then the hole reopens and we feel even more of a tug at our hearts. To say yes to that unsatisfying but unbending truth of impermanence, Buddha's first truth, a lifelong undertaking, is our most enchanting psychological challenge and our most liberating spiritual practice. In our yes to that challenge is a narrow but well-lighted path to the inner shrine of our true self, our enlightened nature. There all our longings abide fulfilled as the quiet qualities of our wholeness. We find the path into it in Psalm 46:10:

"Be still and know." We hear it again from the Gnostic teacher Allogenes: "I found a silent stillness within me and in it was the grace whereby I knew myself as I am." (Nag Hammadi Library) This stillness is a royal road to trust, the link between holding our longings as longings for more and feeling them within us as the riches of enough. We can trust that:

- our longing for love reflects the fact that we are love;
- our longing for meaning reflects our meaningful presence in the world;
- our longing for freedom happens because we are indeed free already and always;
- our longing for happiness reflects the gift of joy so accessible when we live at a heart level;
- our longing for growth is fulfilled in every moment, since we are individual instances of the cosmos evolving in a brilliance that knows no cessation.

In this book we have visited the Manhattan and the Scotland in ourselves, the hard sidewalks and luscious fields of our longings. We found out a little more about what it means to be human—and about how to be human too. That is the question and quest of a lifetime leading only and always to a most radiant Yes. In that yes, desire loses its lure and longing its ache.

> Month by month, things are losing their hardness; even my body now lets the light through.
>
> —VIRGINIA WOOLF, *The Waves*

Appendix: Loving-Kindness Practices

With good will for the entire cosmos, cultivate a limitless heart: above, below, and all around, unobstructed, without enmity or hate.

—Karaniya Metta Sutta, translation by Thanissaro Bhikkhu

In Buddhism there are four immeasurable qualities in our enlightened nature: loving-kindness, compassion, joy, and equanimity. These four attributes are considered immeasurable because the extent to which they can be shown is limitless, as is their contribution to our spiritual development. They are also called the *brahmaviharas,* which means "divine abodes," that which we might call the residence of our Buddha nature. These four qualities represent higher states of consciousness, the wholesome qualities of enlightenment always present in each of us. They are ever-ready potentials, latent energies waiting for activation we can aspire to in daily life. Note that an aspiration *is* a longing, so the four immeasurables are not only qualities of our inner life but longings in us too.

Loving-kindness, the first immeasurable, is meant in the sense of friendliness. When we see suffering in a friendly way, our loving-kindness becomes compassion. When we see others' happiness or success in a friendly way, our loving-kindness becomes shared joy.

When we hold our and others' predicaments in a friendly way, we experience equanimity, which balances and holds the other three. Equanimity also sometimes carries the meaning of giving loving-kindness, compassion, and joy to others universally rather than selectively. We recall George Herbert's poem "The Call" in which he also combines equanimity with happiness and love: "Such a joy as none can move, such a love as none can part."

The loving-kindness, *metta,* practice is how we cultivate the four immeasurables in daily life. We do this by a combination of meditation and action. In the meditation practice, we state internally or verbally that we aspire to each of the four, first for ourselves, then for our near and dear, then for people who are neutral to us, then for those we dislike or have difficulty with, and finally for all beings.

Loving-kindness is the virtue that makes us want ourselves and others to be happy. Our aspiration is: "May I be happy. May those who are dear to me be happy. May those who are neutral to me be happy. May those with whom I have difficulty be happy. May all beings be happy."

Compassion is the attitude that sincerely wishes that all be free of suffering, including ourselves. Our aspiration is: "May I be free of suffering. May those who are dear to me be free of suffering. May those who are neutral to me be free of suffering. May those with whom I have difficulty be free of suffering. May all beings be free of suffering."

Sympathetic joy shows our happiness at others' success, progress, good fortune. We are genuinely happy also for those who have found some fulfillment of the five longings: love, meaning, freedom, happiness, growth. Our aspiration is: "May I be happy about the happiness of others. May those who are dear to me be happy about the happiness of others. May those who are neutral to me be happy about the happiness of others. May those with whom I have difficulty be happy about the happiness of others. May all beings be happy about the happiness of one another."

Equanimity is a mature attitude toward pleasure and pain, an ability to handle what happens without an undermining distress. It is also an even-minded response to what happens, a composure in the midst of any predicament. In this way of seeing it, we have equanimity when we are serene about what we cannot change. We expand our equanimity when we are animated and courageous about what we can change and have the wisdom to know and act on the difference. All this adds up to being appropriate in our feelings, which is another way of describing equanimity. Our aspiration is: "May I be even tempered and appropriate in my feelings no matter what happens. May those who are dear to me be even tempered and appropriate in their feelings no matter what happens. May those who are neutral to me be even tempered and appropriate in their feelings no matter what happens. May those with whom I have difficulty be even tempered and appropriate in their feelings no matter what happens. May all beings be even tempered and appropriate in their feelings no matter what happens."

As an alternative practice of loving-kindness, we can use the following four wishes for well-being to ourselves and others: happiness, safety, health, and peace.

By moving in this meditation from focusing on ourselves to focusing on others, our hearts become concentric circles of stronger and stronger connection. This is another path to freedom from the illusion that we exist as separate.

The metta practice also includes action. We act with loving-kindness, show compassion when others suffer, show joy when others are happy, show equanimity in all our reactions and predicaments. We are moving from aspiration to commitment to a spiritually awakened way of living.

Reciprocal inhibition is used as a psychological term that correlates with the Buddhist phrase *antidote practice*. We do the opposite of what we want to cease doing. We hold the positive as an antidote to the negative. For instance, we want to free ourselves from arrogance, so we show humility. The new behavior, humility, cannot coexist with arrogance, so we gradually free ourselves from its grip. Indeed, each of the four immeasurables helps free us from its opposite: loving-kindness opposes and ends ill will and aggression.

Compassion opposes and ends cold indifference to suffering or seeing those who suffer as one-down from us. Our sympathetic joy counters envy, selfishness, and resentment. Equanimity offsets reactiveness and the fear behind it—which can lead to clinging or compulsion, the charioteers of suffering.

Here are daily affirmations that reflect the four immeasurables:

> May I show all the love I have, here, now, and all the time.
> May I show compassion to everyone in pain.
> May I be joyful about the good that happens to any of us.
> May I respond with equanimity to all that happens.

> One by one, Lord, I see and I love all those whom you have given me to sustain and charm my life. One by one . . . I call before me the whole vast anonymous army of living humanity . . . who today will take up again their impassioned pursuit of the light.
>
> —Pierre Teilhard de Chardin, *Hymn of the Universe*

Loving-Kindness and the Five Longings

We can create our own loving-kindness practice using the five longings as we would the four immeasurables. We can aspire for ourselves and others that we all find love, meaning, freedom, happiness, and growth in our daily life. We take them one at a time, in that order. Our meditation practice may begin like this:

> May I be loving and loved.
> May I see a meaning in all that happens.
> May I be free.
> May I be happy.
> May I find ways to grow from all that happens to me.

As in the standard metta practice, we then apply each of the above aspirations in turn to those we care about, to those neutral to us, to those we have difficulty with, and to all beings.

We end our meditation by honoring the place within us where all of us already and always have the same five inner riches. We acknowledge love, meaning, freedom, happiness, and growth as qualities of our Buddha nature like the four immeasurables. For this we express gratitude.

We round out our meditative practice with new behaviors. We commit ourselves to act in ways that foster some fulfillment of the five longings in ourselves and others:

- We show and are open to love.
- We make meaningful choices and look for meaning in life events.
- We keep freeing ourselves from fear, inhibition, control, and compulsion.
- We do what leads to happiness for ourselves and others.
- We commit ourselves to consciously evolving, to finding growth-openings in all events and relationships.

WORKING WITH OUR OBSESSIVE, JUDGMENTAL, OR WORRISOME THOUGHTS

> The greatest weapon against stress is our ability to choose one thought over another.
>
> —WILLIAM JAMES

Here is a technique I have devised and am now using. It began with my reading about an experience of Saint Thérèse of Lisieux, a late nineteenth-century French Carmelite nun. A thought of someone would come to her while she was praying. At first she disciplined herself to put the thought aside and return to her prayer. Later, she found a new response: She simply offered the prayer *for* the person she had just thought of. Perhaps the person who came to Saint Thérèse's mind in that moment needed her prayers—if synchronicity was at work.

I am applying this style to the times when I find myself having obsessive or judgmental thoughts about someone or a worry about something. Now, instead of indulging the thoughts or acting on them, I immediately begin doing metta for the person or for those in any way connected to the worry, including me. I am noticing that when I voice-over the aggressive or scary thoughts about someone or some impending event with the words of loving-kindness, I really do free myself from obsession and negativity. I also notice I feel less afraid. The repetitive nature of obsession and resentments is what makes them endure. The repetitive use of this practice as an immediate response also lays down new neural pathways out of the obsession, aggression, and fear. I am now reprogramming my brain/body from fear-based to love-based habit patterns, from negative thoughts to positive ones, from aggressive reactions to compassionate responses. I am placing my mind's obsessions, antagonisms, and anxieties into a heart space and that releases me from their grip. My human nature is aligned to my Buddha nature. It is so consoling to realize that I always have recourse to the practice of loving-kindness—anywhere, anytime, in any relationship, in any predicament.

Finally, we can also apply this practice to recurrent memories, especially the ones associated with unresolved issues or troubling emotions. The practice does not take the place of our psychological work, but it does supplement it.

I say Yes to everything that happens to me today
as an opportunity
to give and receive love without reserve.
I am thankful for the enduring capacity to love
that has come to me from the Sacred Heart of the universe.
May everything that happens to me today
open my heart more and more.
May all that I think, say, feel, and do express loving-kindness
toward myself, those close to me, and all beings.
May love be my life purpose, my bliss, my calling, my destiny,

the richest grace I can receive or give.
And may I always be especially compassionate
toward people who are considered least or last
or who feel alone or lost.

THE PRACTICE OF FORGIVENESS

A largess universal, like the sun,
His liberal eye doth give to everyone.
SHAKESPEARE, *Henry V*

Another element of loving-kindness is forgiveness. We begin with a look at definitions:

Forgive: "to remit an offense or debt, to absolve, to give up all claim on, to cease to feel resentment against, for example, to forgive one's enemies."

Pardon: "to release someone from the consequences and penalties that attach to an offense."

We see the difference: To pardon is an action in response to an offender; to forgive is an attitude in the offended person that entails freedom from negative reactions toward the offender. Pardon is for the benefit of the offender; forgiveness benefits the offender and the offended one.

Regarding finding pardon: An offense, legal or personal, leads to a need for amends. We pay the consequences and have thereby paid our debt to society or to a person. We can also be pardoned by the goodwill of a judge or any person without having to pay any penalty.

Regarding finding forgiveness: An offense, criminal or personal, can lead to a grudge in the one who was offended or victimized. That person reacts with blame, resentment, hate, and the need to retaliate. Forgiveness is letting go of those reactions. We can ask for amends or not. Forgiveness is a new inner attitude. To pardon helps the other; to forgive helps us first, then the other.

Neither pardoning nor forgiving mean condoning or excusing, nor do they mean allowing offenses to continue. Both pardon and forgiveness are about letting go of reactions and consequences, not at all about letting offenses continue.

We can pardon at will, but we can't make ourselves forgive. Forgiveness simply happens. The difference between a doing and a happening is like the difference between acting lovingly and falling in love. We can do what it takes to act in a loving way, but we cannot make ourselves fall in love. That has to happen; it is not in the realm of choice or willpower. It is a grace of synchronicity.

So then how do we open to the grace of forgiveness? How do we hold the intention and make the choices that help us move toward forgiveness? Here is a six-part practice that has worked for me and others:

1. Whenever you are offended or hurt, let yourself first grieve the pain, that is, feel your feelings of sadness and anger. The refusal to forgive is first of all a refusal to grieve, which is the experience that best leads to letting go. We recall Shakespeare's *Troilus and Cressida:* "Hope of revenge shall hide our inward woe."

2. Ask for or open to the grace to let go of hate, resentment, and revenge. Forgiveness is nothing less than letting go of these three unskillful ego reactions to experiences of hurt and unfairness. Forgiveness is a release from the long-standing aggression in our indignant ego, which kills our lively energy with hateful, resentful, and retaliatory thoughts and plans.

3. Abstain from acting on the hate, resentment, and retaliation. We can't make ourselves let go of these as thoughts, but we do have control over how we ultimately choose to act. Gradually, our thoughts become more gentle as a result.

4. Imagine that you are holding the memory of the hurt in your generous heart, not in your affronted ego. This is holding the intention to forgive the specific people who have offended you. It is a shift from exclusion to inclusion. We hold those who have hurt us as in a locket, not as locked out.

5. Say yes to the given of life that people are sometimes mean or unfair and may disappoint, hurt, or betray you. This is accepting the reality of the human shadow, and we can now do so with compassion:

> We were taught to harm those who hate us.
> *We have it in us to do good to those who hate us.*
> We were taught to curse those who curse us.
> *We have it in us to bless and wish the best for those who curse us.*
> We were taught to get back at those who mistreat us.
> *We have it in us to pray for or wish for enlightenment for those who mistreat us.*

Our affirmations, based on Luke 6:27–28, are:

- May I do good to those who hate me.
- May I bless those who curse me.
- May I pray for (or wish enlightenment to) those who mistreat me.

6. Continually affirm the attitude of forgiveness by daily use of this practice paraphrased from Buddhist teaching:

- I ask forgiveness for all the ways I have harmed others.
- I am open to the grace to forgive those who have harmed me.
- I forgive myself for any ways I have harmed myself.

Hatred does not cease by hatred, only by love; this is the eternal commandment.

—Dhammapada

About the Author

David Richo, PhD, MFT, is a psychotherapist and workshop leader who lives in Santa Barbara and San Francisco, California. He combines Jungian, Buddhist, and mythic perspectives in his work. Dave is the author of the following books and audios:

How to Be an Adult: A Handbook on Psychological and Spiritual Integration (Paulist Press, 1991)

Happy, mature people have somehow picked up the knack of being generous with their sympathies while still taking care of themselves. We can all evolve from the neurotic ego through a healthy ego to the spiritual self. We can deal with fear, anger, and guilt. We can be assertive, have boundaries, and build intimacy.

When Love Meets Fear: Becoming Defense-less and Resource-full (Paulist Press, 1997)

Our lively energy is inhibited by fear, and we are so often needlessly on the defensive. We consider the origins and healing of our fears of closeness, commitment, aloneness, and assertiveness, and of panic attacks. We can free ourselves from the grip of fear so that it no longer stops or drives us.

Shadow Dance: Liberating the Power and Creativity of Your Dark Side (Shambhala Publications, 1999)

The shadow is all that we abhor about ourselves as well as all the dazzling potential that we doubt or deny we have. We project these on to others as dislike or admiration. We can acknowledge our limitations and our gifts. Then both our light and our dark sides become sources of creativity and grant us access to our untapped inner wealth.

How to Be an Adult in Relationships: The Five Keys to Mindful Loving (Shambhala Publications, 2002)

Love is not so much a feeling as a way of being present. Love is presence with these five *A*'s: unconditional attention, acceptance, appreciation, affection, and allowing others to be as they are. Love is presence without the five conditioned overlays of ego: judgment, fear, control, attachment, and illusion.

The Five Things We Cannot Change: And the Happiness We Find by Embracing Them (Shambhala Publications, 2005)

There are unavoidable "givens" in life and relationships. By our unconditional yes to these conditions of existence, we learn to open, accept, even embrace our predicaments without trying to control the outcomes. We begin to trust what happens as gifts of grace that help us grow in character, depth, and compassion.

The Power of Coincidence: How Life Shows Us What We Need to Know (Shambhala Publications, 2007)

There are meaningful coincidences of events, dreams, or relationships that happen to us beyond our control. These synchronicities influence the course of our life in mysterious ways. They often reveal assisting forces that are pointing us to our unguessed, unexpected, and unimagined destiny.

The Sacred Heart of the World: Restoring Mystical Devotion to Our Spiritual Life (Paulist Press, 2007)

We explore the symbolism of the heart in world religious traditions and then trace the historical thread of Christian devotion to the Sacred Heart of Jesus into modern times. We focus on the philosophy and theology of Pierre Teilhard de Chardin and Karl Rahner to design a new sense of what devotion can be.

Wisdom's Way: Quotations for Meditation (Human Development Books, 2008)

This is a book of quotations from a variety of sources, especially Buddhist, Christian, Jungian, and transpersonal. The quotations are brief and can be used as springboards for meditation. They are divided into three sections: psychological insight, spiritual awareness, and mystical realization.

Making Love Last: How to Sustain Intimacy and Nurture Genuine Connection (set of 3 CDs or available as MP3 download, Shambhala Publications, 2008)

Here is a lively workshop given by David Richo at Spirit Rock, a Buddhist retreat center in California, on relationship issues. These are some of the topics: how love can endure, fears of intimacy and commitment, trust and fidelity, resolving our conflicts, the phases of a relationship, how our early life affects our adult relationships.

When the Past Is Present: Healing the Emotional Wounds That Sabotage Our Relationships (Shambhala Publications, 2008)

Transference is a tendency to see our parents or other significant characters in our life story in others. We explore how our past impacts our present relationships. We find ways to make transference a valuable opportunity to learn about ourselves, deepen our relationships, and heal our ancient wounds.

Being True to Life: Poetic Paths to Personal Growth (Shambhala Publications, 2009)

Poetry may have seemed daunting in school, but here is a chance for it to become quite wonderfully personal and spiritually enriching. This book offers an opportunity to use our hearts and pens to release the full range of our imagination and discover ourselves through reading and writing poetry.

Daring to Trust: Opening Ourselves to Real Love and Intimacy (Shambhala Publications, 2010)

We learn how to build trust, how to recognize a trustworthy person, how to work with our fears around trusting, and how to rebuild trust after a breach or infidelity. We find ways to trust others, to trust ourselves, to trust reality, to trust what happens to us, and to trust a higher power than ourselves.

How to Be an Adult in Faith and Spirituality (Paulist Press, 2011)

We explore and compare religion and spirituality, with an emphasis on how they can both become rich resources for personal growth. We increase our understanding of God, faith, and life's plaguing questions in the light of mysticism, depth psychology, and our new appreciation of evolutionary cosmology.

How to Be an Adult in Faith and Spirituality (set of 4 CDs or available as MP3 download, Paulist Press, 2012)

This set of CDs from a workshop given at Spirit Rock, a Buddhist retreat center in California, is about how to design and practice an adult spirituality. We also learn to find the archetypal riches in religion and cherish them. We let go of what is not in keeping with our adult growth, both psychologically and spiritually.

Coming Home to Who You Are: Discovering Your Natural Capacity for Love, Integrity, and Compassion (Shambhala Publications, 2011)

Here are practices that can usher us into a new way of being alive—as cheerful agents of the goodness that is in all of us. Our choices for integrity and loving-kindness reflect that goodness and help us cocreate a world of justice, peace, and love. This is an owner's guide to being an upright and loving human.

How to Be an Adult in Love: Letting Love in Safely and Showing It Recklessly (Shambhala Publications, 2013)

We explore ways to love ourselves without guilt and with generosity. We learn how to love others with awareness of our boundaries. We confront our fears of love and loving. We embrace the spiritual challenge of letting the range of our love expand. Then love is a force for caring connection—unconditional, universal, and jubilant.

Embracing the Shadow: Discovering the Hidden Riches in Our Relationships (set of 4 CDs, Shambhala Publications, 2013)

We work with our unskillful tendencies in our relationships so that we can tame them and grow because of them. We notice our projections onto one another. We find the gifts we might not yet have dared to recognize or show. Working *with* the dark rather than *in* it lets the light of intimacy through. This set of CDs is from a workshop given at Spirit Rock, a Buddhist retreat center in California.

Meaningful Coincidence: A Workshop on Synchronicity in Relationships and the Events That Shape Our Lives (downloads from Shambhala Publications, not on CDs)

How to Be an Adult in Relationships: The Five Keys to Mindful Loving (read by the author; Shambhala Publications, 2013; CDs or available as MP3 download)

The Power of Grace: Recognizing Unexpected Gifts on Our Path (Shambhala Publications, 2014)

If we think back over our life and relationships, we notice benefits that came to us beyond our effort, plan, or expectation. That special assistance, unearned, unforeseen, unplanned, often unnoticed, is grace, the gift dimension of life. We cannot make it happen, but we can open to it and be conduits of it.

When Catholic Means Cosmic: Opening to a Big-Hearted Faith (Paulist Press, 2015)

When Catholic has cosmic dimensions, we and our religion expand: We update our beliefs in accord with advances in psychology and science. We appreciate the traditional riches of our religion while being contemporary too. People of all traditions will find this book helpful since we explore how religion and spirituality can be integrated.

You Are Not What You Think: The Egoless Path to Self-Esteem and Generous Love (Shambhala Publications, 2015)

Egotism can get in the way of self-development, successful relation-ships, and spiritual growth. We can look at the "big ego" in our-selves and others not with disdain but with compassion. We can tame our own ego so that it contributes to our self-esteem. The ego we let go of is replaced by the ego we grow by.

When Mary Becomes Cosmic: A Jungian and Mystical Path to the Divine Feminine (Paulist Press, 2016)

Our vision of Mary can become cosmic in scope. The Jungian arche-type of the divine feminine as personified by Mary is built into the design of every human psyche. Her ancient titles reflect the marvel-ous qualities of our essential Self. In fact, every religious truth and image is a metaphor for potentials in us and in the universe.

For more information, including videos on YouTube, upcoming events, and a catalog of audio programs, visit davericho.com.